THE
Simon Peter
PRINCIPLES

How an impetuous, faltering disciple was changed into a great servant for God

Keith S. Hodges

Keith S Hodges
2018

The Simon Peter Principles
by Keith S. Hodges
© 2007

ISBN 978-1981915651

Star Bible
www.starbible.com

Dedication

To my parents, Lee and Kay Hodges – You have been watching me "stumble forward" longer than anyone else. Thanks for everything!

Acknowledgements

I am indebted to many Christian friends who through the years have encouraged me to write. My wife, Francie, was most patient with me during this writing and the ordeals of getting it published – Thanks Dear! My parents read every word, section by section, as it was being written, offering many helpful suggestions. Special thanks to my sister, Jenna Wise, who offered feedback, along with other readers who made invaluable contributions throughout the process: Molly Keener, Shelley Baumgarten, Dr. Don Flatt, and Dr. Bill Bowen. I also received great advice and encouragement from two accomplished authors, Dr. Tom Olbricht and Jim Woodroof. (Jim dubbed me "the king of split infinitives." I'm glad he made me aware that the way I speak doesn't come across as well on paper!) Other Christian friends who gave me special encouragement through this period included Bob Lang, Dr. JoEllen Halteman, Paul Fisher, Dr. Beverly Niehls and Chip Hartzell.

And finally, the entire Chesmont Church, who for the last 12 years has heard or seen most of this material in sermons, classes, and bulletin articles – you folks were a great sounding board!

Introduction

I have more than just a passing interest in this man, Simon Peter, and his life. Years ago a trusted friend (an elder in the church, and a practicing psychologist) casually told me in a conversation, "Keith, you're a lot like the Apostle Peter!" Well, was I to take that as a compliment or a rebuke? It was a compliment if he meant I was strong in faith, courageous, and a natural leader. But it wasn't so flattering if he meant I was pride-filled, impetuous, and short-tempered. (I suspect it was more of the latter than the former!)

With that comparison to the Apostle Peter echoing in the back of my mind, I began to take notice of this most fascinating and, I would soon realize, compelling character. I found him to be at times funny, annoying, insightful, dense, and usually by the end of a particular story from his life, quite endearing.

Whether we want to admit it or not, there's a little "Simon Peter" in all of us. I believe that very fact, how each of us can relate to him in some way or another, is why he is singled out noticeably more than any of the other apostles in the gospel accounts.

Jesus didn't stop calling disciples when He concluded his mission on Earth and returned to his Father. He still calls for people to follow Him and imitate Him today. But the truth is each one will have to go through his or her own growing pains as a disciple, just like Simon Peter did. Let's learn from our fellow-disciple, Simon Peter, as we learn from the Master, Jesus.

Keith S. Hodges, 2007

"Grace and peace be yours in abundance." (1st Peter 1:2)

Table of Contents

d. Simon, Are You Sleeping?

PRINCIPLE SEVEN – Learning From Failures is the Best Way to Become a Success

a. A Different Kind Of Barber
b. Ol' "Wavering Rock" Personified
c. The Look
d. Bitter Tears

PRINCIPLE EIGHT – God Doesn't Want You to Quit Just Because You Failed

a. Go Tell Peter
b. Seeing Is (Not Always) Believing
c. He Was Willing To Hang Out The 'Gone Fishin' Sign
d. Another Big Fish Tale

PRINCIPLE NINE – God's Restoration Process Is Necessary

a. Do You Really Love Me, Simon?
b. Feed The Sheep
c. What about Him?
d. Simon Peter Uses "The Keys" For The First Time

PRINCIPLE TEN – Hang in Long Enough and You'll Begin to Succeed

a. What I Have, I Give You
b. The First Arrest
c. Simon Peter, The Prosecuting Attorney
d. Power in His Shadow (!)

PRINCPLE ELEVEN – Never Assume You've Grown Enough

a. Simon Peter On The Subject of Obedience
b. Simon Peter The Missionary
c. Simon Peter Ministering Here And There
d. Another Lesson For Simon Peter To Learn

PRINCIPLE TWELVE - Be Prepared For Anything

a. Don't Worship Me!
b. Simon Peter Uses "The Keys" To Open The Way To Gentiles

c. Another Arrest, And A Miraculous Deliverance
d. Growth Is An Exciting Thing To See

PRINCPLE THIRTEEN – Keep Striving And Maturity Will Come

a. Simon Peter Knew Something Of Grace
b. Another Rebuke
c. Kind Words For Paul
d. Be Sure You Remember

PRINCIPLE ONE

"You Never Know When God Is Going To Call"

a. "Well, How Do You Make Disciples?"

READ **Matthew 28:16-20**

Twelve men met on a mountain in Galilee. Eleven of the men were summoned by the twelfth. All of them had some things in common, but the twelfth was extraordinarily different than the rest. Specifically, He was recently killed, and then miraculously raised from the dead. The twelfth man was, of course, Jesus Christ, the Son of God. The others were his apostles. Before being selected as apostles, the men had been a part of a larger company of disciples (followers, imitators) of Jesus. For several years they had traveled with Him, hearing Him teach, watching Him interact with people in all kinds of situations, and seeing Him perform various miracles.

Since His resurrection Jesus had appeared to the eleven and many others. But they were still amazed. When they met Him on the mountain, they worshipped Him. But even at this point, the text plainly says, "Some doubted."

Then Jesus gave them their marching orders, which has been dubbed "the great commission." The sum of this charge was given on several different occasions (see Mark 16:15,16, Luke 24:46-50, Acts 1:8). When they had received all His instruction in this regard, He would amaze them one last time by ascending into the skies before their very eyes.

But let's go back to the meeting on the mountain, where one of those present was Simon Peter. He needed no explanation of what it meant to "make disciples," for that's what Jesus had been doing with him for over three years. The theme of this book is the struggle associated with being a disciple of Jesus Christ. It is not surprising, therefore, that Simon Peter is the main character.

Next to Jesus Christ, Simon Peter is the person most mentioned in the Gospels. In the book of Acts he was the first prominent leader in the early church and was observed to be one of those "unschooled, ordinary men" (Acts 4:13) whose lives had been turned upside down by knowing Jesus and who then helped turned the world upside down for Christ.

Simon Peter was something of an enigma. He was alternately courageous, cowardly, brilliant, dull, strong and weak. Some of his most shining moments were followed, often almost immediately, by some of his greatest personal failures. Let's be honest – his most pronounced characteristic was his tendency to be impetuous. He surely had the worst case of Foot in Mouth disease in recorded history. His career as a disciple and apostle could be characterized as stumbling forward. Yet with all these tendencies, there is something honest and compelling about this man and his story.

The business world has its "Peter Principle," a theory introduced by author Lawrence J. Peter in the late 1960s. It suggests people in a business or organization tend to rise (either by self-striving or promotion) just beyond where they best function. The phrase "the Peter Principle" is often used with a negative connotation – a put down, not a compliment.

Coincidentally, some might see the "Peter Principle" in the person of Simon Peter. Not so! As unlikely a candidate for greatness as he was, he was able to get beyond himself in a positive way: with the Lord's help, Simon Peter became more than he, or any who knew him, could have ever imagined.

This book looks at Simon Peter's life through his personality traits, strengths, weaknesses, and most importantly, his heart. Modern-day disciples can learn a lot from the fisherman who followed Jesus.

Jesus is our example, our ultimate role model. We are to keep our eyes trained on Him (Hebrews 12:2ff), and ever be imitating Him. Yet for some, Simon Peter is the one in Jesus' story with whom they can most easily relate. Perhaps watching Simon Peter evolve as a man of faith will make it easier to "grow in the grace and knowledge of our Lord and Savior Jesus Christ" (2 Peter 3:18).

I was the preacher for a church planting in the Northeast. Our growing congregation had an active outreach, but we had never seen anyone like Joe. A recent convert himself, he found us. He and a small band of his friends were spontaneously conducting Bible studies in a park, in their homes, and just about anywhere else anyone would listen to them. Joe was the definite leader. Frequently he would call me telling me someone had decided to become a Christian. But there was one problem. Many of these new converts didn't stay involved long enough to even come to church the following Sunday. Few kept their commitment longer than a month. In the practical sense, the mortality rate of these "babes in Christ" was alarming. It was apparent Joe had a knack for sharing with people the message of salvation. But the message of commitment and growth in Christ was sorely lacking. I asked Joe to meet with me for a Bible study. We studied the "great commission." We reviewed the four main points of Jesus' charge – going, making disciples, baptizing, and ongoing teaching. Then I shared with Joe that Greek scholars say one of these four is an imperative verb and thus carries the real "punch" of the message. The other three, though essential to the overall plan, are actually participles to that imperative verb. Then I asked him which one he thought was the imperative verb.

Joe immediately blurted out "baptizing!" "No," I said, "try again." He studied the text for a moment and said "Going, you've got to always be going." I shook my head no. Then he looked at the text for an even longer time before reaching up and slapping his forehead as the answer dawned on him. "The 'teaching them to continue' – that's what you're always telling me I need to do, right?" But I replied, "That's not it." With only one possible choice left, he said quietly and almost in disbelief, "Making disciples?" And I nodded yes.

I shall never forget what happened next. To his great credit Joe humbly asked, "Well, how do you make disciples?" He was now wide open for teaching. In the ensuing months, the number of baptisms decreased, but the number of disciples staying with us dramatically increased.

Are you a disciple of Jesus Christ? If so, are you allowing the process of discipleship to continue? Also, do you know how to "make disciples," as Jesus commanded? These are lifelong challenges for those of us who have determined to follow the Lord. Our discipleship has to be rooted in knowledge of Jesus from the Scriptures. But within that larger study is the fascinating subplot of Simon Peter, one who struggled and eventually gained the victory in this regard!

"Simon Peter, a servant and apostle of Jesus Christ, to those who through the righteousness of our God and Savior Jesus Christ have received a faith as precious as ours . . . ." (2nd Peter 1:1)

4

b. What's In a Name?

READ **John 1:42**

Simon Peter was a man of several names! His given name was Simon, and he is introduced to us as "Simon Bar-jona," "Simon Son of Jona," or "Simon, son of John," as related in several references and depending on which version you're reading.

Simon was a fairly common name in first century Palestine. It also occurs as "Simeon." One of Jesus' half-brothers was named Simon (Mark 6:3; Matthew 13:55). But what most folks don't realize is that Simon may not have been a particularly flattering name. It originally meant, "wavering one," and was sometimes given to children who demonstrated a hesitant or indecisive spirit. Sometimes the Jews, much like Native Americans, often waited a while to name their children. (Contrast this with the angels' pre-birth declarations of names for John and Jesus.) We're not sure if our Simon received his name as a namesake for some family member or friend, or if indeed he displayed a 'back and forth' tendency as a child. A few years ago a popular American movie had two key characters. Both were of European descent, but had come to live with a tribe of Sioux Indians. The tribe named the man Dances with Wolves, and the woman he married had been named Stands with a Fist. Both names were based on actions observed by the Native Americans. If your parents had waited two or three years to name you, what might your name be?

It was Simon Peter's brother Andrew who introduced him to Jesus. It is not clear from the passages in the early part of the Gospels whether or not Simon was a disciple of John the Baptist, but Simon's brother and fishing partner Andrew was, and he was one of the two who heard John say, "Look, the Lamb of God!" They literally follow Jesus, talk with Him, and end up spending the day with Him. Apparently convinced that Jesus was somebody special, the text says, "The first thing Andrew did was to find his brother Simon," and he proclaimed "We have found the Messiah."

Though this book is about Simon Peter, let's notice something about Simon's brother Andrew. Except for being mentioned in the several lists of apostles, Andrew is only mentioned three times in the New Testament, all by the writer John. The pairs of brothers, Simon and Andrew, and James and John, were partners in the fishing business. It seems only natural that John, writing years later, would remember and call attention to some of Andrew's actions that the other Gospel writers might not include.

5

One of the major themes of this book will focus on the impetuous nature of Simon Peter. Andrew may have been entirely different. That's good to notice. For while some of us may relate more to the impetuous Simon Peter, some of you less-impetuous types may not relate to him so well at all. That's fine, because just like Jesus picked the twelve with a variety of backgrounds, He surely picked men with a variety of personality traits as well. The same is true today. People can have any number of different personal traits – whichever ones the Lord gave them – and still be effective in their service to Him.

In each of the three passages where Andrew is mentioned, he shows himself to be something of a "people-person." First, he goes and gets his brother Simon to introduce him to Jesus. In John chapter 6 where Jesus has decided to feed the multitude that has been listening to Him teach, the other disciples are wondering how they'll be able to afford such a feeding, but it is Andrew who has found (or been found by) a boy with loaves and fishes. Finally, in John chapter 12, it is Andrew who is a "middle man" in the process of getting people to Jesus. Some Greeks have told Philip they want to see Jesus. Philip tells Andrew, who in turn tells Jesus.

Andrew is what might be called a "quiet evangelist." He isn't one who calls a lot of attention to himself – he just gets the job done! We need many of this type of people in the church. For example, they are the ones who can get their friends to come to church, where someone else can complete the job of teaching.

Now back to Simon. Let's consider the first time Jesus ever saw him. (Please notice and don't forget that the text says Jesus "looked at him.") The Lord declares he will be called Cephas, or Peter. Both names mean "rock" from their respective languages. Cephas is from Aramaic, the everyday language of Palestine. Peter is from Greek, the universal language of that time, and the language in which the New Testament would be written years later.

At first it seems like an odd thing for Jesus to meet a man and nickname him "rock." The fuller meaning is going to become clearer in a later episode. But in the meantime you have a man with a name that is an oxymoron (a self-contradicting phrase). Meet "Wavering Rock." Jesus did not name him "rock" for what he was, but what he would become through the grace of God.

The name sticks. So throughout the rest of the Biblical references to him, he's alternately called Simon, Simon Peter, Peter, or Cephas. Ironically, after giving him the nickname, which the various writers frequently use, Jesus only refers to him once as Peter (Luke 22:34). Otherwise Jesus calls him Simon. Later in life Peter would write two books, and in one refer to himself as Simon Peter and in the other simply as Peter.

Now that you know this little "name game" for yourself, watch how often our subject is acting more like a "wavering one," more like a "rock," or usually a weird combination of the two!

I've had several nicknames, but none that has stuck with me for life (at least not yet!). My first nickname was "little Bud," because I so carefully imitated the walk and other actions of my grandfather, Paul "Bud" Scott. While playing college basketball, I was called "Stick," because I was painfully skinny. But the idea of having a nickname based on a spiritual trait might be downright intimidating! We'd like to think we'd have an honorable nickname like Joseph in Acts chapter 4 whom the apostles called Barnabas, which means "son of encouragement." If Jesus were to look you or me in the eye right now, what nickname might he give us?

You won't have the opportunity to be given a new name by Jesus today. You probably won't even get one from your local church. But you do have a name. And the mention of that name will eventually fall as either pleasant or painful on the ears of those who know you. They'll know you for your devotion and service or lack thereof. It's a fact of life: we make a name for ourselves, one-way or the other. Decide to live in such a way as to always do honor to your name. And more importantly, do honor to the name Christian, which means "little Christ."

"However, if you suffer as a Christian, do not be ashamed, but praise God that you bear that name." (1st Peter 4:16)

c. A Blue-collar Disciple

READ **Matthew 4:18-22; Mark 1:16-20**

If you had been Jesus, looking for a spiritual leader to carry on your work in just a few years, where would you have conducted your search? Would you have looked among the priests? Or at the Sanhedrin, the political-religious high court of the day? Perhaps you'd search at one of the rabbinical schools, the seminaries of that day? Probably the last place you would look would be at the docks among fishermen. Even if Simon Peter was, as some believe, a successful businessman, we still don't know if he had much formal education. But Jesus didn't go looking for potential apostles among the academic elite or the professional religionists, at least at this point. (Years later He would select Paul, a highly educated religious leader, as an additional apostle.)

Jesus, being God in the flesh, could see a man for more than what he was at the moment. He could see his potential. "Man looks on the outward appearance; God looks at the heart" (1 Samuel 16:7).

It's easy to get confused with the timetable, but somewhere from a few months to as much as a year-and-a-half may have passed from when the Lord and Simon first met and when he became an active disciple of Jesus. So Simon Peter had a while to let it all soak in. Meanwhile, he had continued his career as a fisherman.

We know Simon Peter had to be a rugged individual. Like today, both professional fishermen and carpenters (like Jesus) in Palestine had to possess a certain degree of strength, endurance, and skill.

Sometimes people tend to have a rather narrowly defined idea of what type of person might be a likely candidate for ministry. Those with jobs more physical in nature, like fishermen, might be seen as lacking certain capacities necessary for spiritual work. In contrast, a successful businessman might be deemed too aggressive. Both views are grossly unfair – stereotyping at its worst! Let's remember that the disciples who later became apostles included at least four fishermen, a tax collector, a political zealot, and no telling what else! Simon Peter had a lot of rough edges, but not necessarily because of his chosen profession.

I get a little amused at how I ended up being a preacher. It wasn't because there had been any preachers in our immediate family. In fact, I remember as a boy it was suggested to me that someday I might be a preacher and I was adamant in my objection to that idea. I'm sometimes asked if I was "called" into the ministry. If you mean was there a bright light and a booming voice, well, no. If you mean was there interest in spiritual things, providential timing and circumstances, and particularly a few key people who influenced me in that direction, well, then, yes.

I was planning on working as a teacher and coach, but the Lord obviously had other plans. We humans often think of ourselves in terms of what we used to do or how we used to be, and can be slow to recognize or accept what God may be wanting us to do now. One of my favorite non-Biblical sayings is "God is not as interested in your past as He is in your future!" Jesus, a carpenter, chose men from a variety of careers to be his special agents in the world. Later he added another, Paul, who at times supported himself by working as a tentmaker after he became an apostle. Some of Paul's fellow tentmakers were an evangelistic-minded couple named Aquila and Priscilla; the Lord moved them from Rome to Corinth to Ephesus.

God has his own purposes in having us where we are, doing what we're doing. Some spend their whole lives in one place, serving God in their chosen career. Others serve in a variety of locations and vocations. None of this indicates God loves one more than another any more than he loves some more by giving them certain gifts (talents, abilities). There is great contentment in knowing you are doing your best for God where you are today and being ready to move tomorrow if that's His call.

People can do wonderful, exceptional things in their lives, especially in their service to God. But many successful people are rather surprised at what they end up doing and how they got there. One of the lessons you'll learn from Simon Peter, if you haven't already learned it elsewhere, is not to aspire for greatness. Even while being something of a natural leader, we never sense him yearning for the spotlight, like some of the other apostles. But his natural gifts perhaps unseen or unnoticed by everyone except Jesus, propelled him to unimagined service in the kingdom of God.

A modern devotional song has the line "I want to be ready when he calls my name!" The way to be ready for whatever the Lord has in mind for you, great or small, is to be faithfully serving where you are. Don't get too locked in imagining the great things you'll do and for which you'll be noticed. Just doing what God has prepared for you will be great enough, whether anybody else notices or not.

"If anyone speaks, he should do it as one speaking the very words of God. If anyone serves, he should do it with the strength God provides, so that in all things God may be praised through Jesus Christ. To him be the glory and the power for ever and ever. Amen." (1st Peter 4:11)

d. The First Big Fish Tale

READ **Luke 5:1-11**

This is the amplified version of Jesus' calling of his first disciples, focusing on Simon Peter. In this incident, as well as a similar one after His resurrection, Jesus amazed the disciples by directing their fishing efforts in such a way as to garner an unusually large catch. But this demonstration of lordship seemed too much for Simon Peter. All too aware of his own shortcomings (sinfulness), he was completely humbled in the presence of such God-likeness. This, no doubt, was one of many incidents that led him to make his monumental confession of Jesus' identity months later.

He falls at Jesus' knees and asks Him to "Go away from me, Lord!" But Jesus does just the opposite. He calls Simon and the others to follow Him, to become His disciples. And Jesus calls them in language they can understand. They had been men catching fish, but now they were to be "fishers of men."

I think Jesus' use of this phrase "fishers of men" was more than just a little play on words. This was Jesus personalizing the mission He had for these men in terms and concepts they could understand. Whatever your chosen vocation or avocation, after you're in it for a little while you tend to start thinking and talking in the lingo of that activity. For example, I played a lot of basketball. Almost without trying, I often explain things in terms related to that sport.

Jesus' very use of the phrase, "I will build my church" (Matthew 16:18) may have been the carpenter in Him coming out. Also He spoke of having a relationship with Him in terms of a yoke (Matthew 11:28-30). Tradition has it that Jesus was a carpenter who made yokes for the oxen in His hometown of Nazareth. Within that tradition is the beautiful notion that Jesus had a sign over His carpentry shop that read, "MY YOKES FIT!" No one knows if that was true, but we have His own promise that "my yoke is easy and my burden is light."

Jesus frequently incorporated other concepts associated with farming into His teaching, which shouldn't surprise us since He ministered in a culture so closely tied to agriculture. So when we think about it, it shouldn't surprise us that Jesus first chose these apostles, and eventually all of us, from the widest possible range of professions and interests.

There's an important point here that we should not miss. God starts with us where we are. Whatever you're good at or interested in, Jesus can take you right there, begin the process of reorienting your life and thinking, and give you a mission for the rest of your life! Don't be surprised if He calls you to a work that utilizes the skills and interests you already have. And as you try to make disciples for Him, work at learning how to relate to others, starting where they are.

In the next chapter we'll further explore this idea of "start where you are." But first please let me make one point. God's starting with us where we are does not mean (as some would fancifully wish) that God accepts us in whatever state He finds us and is content to let us stay there. Some have terribly misapplied a concept of grace that supposes there will never be any reason or call for us to change, grow, improve, etc. This kind of thinking is entirely inconsistent with the Biblical message of a God who takes us where we are and does everything He can to help us reach our absolute potential, in all areas of our lives, but especially for Him.

"Each one should use whatever gift he has received to serve others, faithfully administering God's grace in its various forms." (1st Peter 4:10)

PRINCIPLE TWO

"Start from Where You Are"

a. Simon Peter, the Married Man

READ **Matthew 8:14-17; Mark 1:29-31; Luke 4:38-41**

Simon Peter was married. We know this for three reasons, indicated from various Scriptures. First, these texts from the Gospels tell us of his mother-in-law being healed by Jesus. Second, the apostle Paul, while defending some of his own rights, appeals to the fact that he could, if he chose to, "lead about a wife like the other apostles ... or Cephas," i.e. Simon Peter (1 Corinthians 9:4). Finally, Simon Peter writes to "fellow elders" (1 Peter 5:2). 1 Timothy 3:3 teaches elders "must be the husband of but one wife."

The fact that Simon Peter was married presents some very intriguing practical questions. When Simon Peter was traveling with Jesus and the others, did his wife stay at home, or was she perhaps a part of the women who accompanied them? (See Luke 8:2; we normally think of only the twelve accompanying Jesus, but in reality a much larger entourage, including women, usually traveled with Him). We don't even know the name of Simon Peter's wife, or how many children they had, or those children's names. (Elders must likewise have children.) Where and how were their children raised? And who supplied the income for Simon Peter's family when he stopped working as a fisherman to be an apostle? (Some have suggested that if he had indeed built a successful fishing business, this may have sustained the family through the time he was with Jesus, but financial support during the years of travel as an apostle remains a mystery.)

I've mulled over exactly what Paul meant when he referred to Simon Peter "leading about" his wife in the later years of his apostleship? Some chauvinists might envision a dictatorial husband dragging her from place to place. But this is inconsistent not only generally with the spirit of true Christianity, but specifically with some of the things Simon Peter would later write about the nature of marriage. It is more conceivable he escorted her to these various locations. (Some versions have "be accompanied by a wife.")

Paul wasn't married, but he wrote about it extensively. Simon Peter was married, but just lived it, though he did write briefly and brilliantly about marriage in 1st Peter 3:1-7. There is no reason to doubt the Lord blessed the marriage of Simon Peter and his wife, and provided for their needs.

Somehow seeing Simon Peter as a married man makes it all seem a little more real. It's another way for those of us who are married to relate to some of the human side of the story. At the

13

same time let us never forget that single people did then and do now have a tremendous work in the Kingdom. Like Jesus. Like Paul. And like many we know today.

I'm so thankful to say I've been "leading about" a wife for over 35 years. In those first few years our average stay in a place was about a year-and-a-half. (I was somewhat impetuous, just like someone we're studying!) Then we stayed in two different locations for four years each. We have just moved after having lived in the same house for over twenty-one years.

Let me say something about the wives of spiritual leaders. This would include the wives of elders, deacons, and ministers. There are some general things said about the wives of elders and deacons in 1st Timothy chapter 3. In addition to those qualities, I've decided the main thing a church leader's wife needs to do is simply be a good wife. It's fine if she wants to teach the ladies class, organize the VBS, or direct the clothing room. But if none of those things is "her thing," that's okay, too! If she loves and supports her husband, making a good home for him and the children, she will have fulfilled all that should be expected of her!

The same is true of the wife of any Christian man. And wives should be content with a husband who honors them, just as Simon Peter describes in his letter. Please be sure to read 1st Peter 3:1-7 for his brief but profound statements on marriage.

Being married neither qualified nor disqualified Simon Peter in his work as an apostle. The same principle is true for any of us in our roles in the church. Married Christians will have to make some allowances to honor their marriage covenants (see 1 Corinthians chapter 7). Single Christians will not have the comfort, strength, and encouragement one receives from a loving spouse, but they should have more time and money to devote to the Lord's work. Don't pine away thinking you could really serve the Lord if only you were in the other situation. God can be glorified by your service in either case if you'll let Him lead you.

"Wives, in the same way be submissive to your husbands . . . . Husbands, in the same way be considerate as you live with your wives, and treat them with respect." (1st Peter 3:1,7)

14

b. The First Sign of Impetuousness

READ **Mark 1:36, 37**

Simon Peter probably didn't intend to be impetuous; it just happened naturally. It was deeply implanted in his nature, as much a part of him as the color of his hair or his eyes. What could have been an annoying trait to most, Jesus apparently saw as his greatest asset. However impulsive, however misguided by wrong-headed thinking, Simon Peter still always wanted to do the right thing!

The question is often asked "Are leaders born or made?" The answer is both! Potential leaders are born with certain unmistakable traits, one of them being impetuousness. Then as part of their change into a good leader, their impetuousness becomes passion for the cause or principles to which they are committed.

Jesus was out early praying. (A lot of your success in ministry can be shaped by what you do with your early mornings.) Simon Peter and his companions came saying, "Everyone is looking for you." Perhaps Simon Peter wants to promote his new hero. Just think of the possibilities! Jesus could set up shop right here in Simon Peter's house. But Jesus had other plans, a bigger mission.

You can say, "Well Simon Peter should have learned right then and there not to jump ahead and make plans for Jesus." Oh, you must not be the impetuous type if you say such a thing! The impetuous person will always assume he or she has a better idea, sees things just a little clearer, or knows exactly what's best for everyone else.

Having been impetuous at least several thousand times in my life, I have something to say about this tendency. If you share this tendency, then you can relate totally. If you don't, then you probably are annoyed at people like us who act this way most of the time. At certain times, particularly in a conversation or class, I feel like I'm going to burst if I don't say something. I honestly don't think and certainly hope it's not arrogance. I know I'm not the sharpest knife in the drawer or the brightest bulb on the Christmas tree – it's just at that particular moment, I want to say something, to make my contribution to the situation at hand. One of my Dad's favorite sayings is "It is better to keep your mouth shut and be thought a fool, than to open it and let out all doubt!" That's a hard lesson for some of us to learn, as it apparently was for Simon Peter. But learn it eventually, we must!

Many new converts to Christ are a bit impetuous in sharing their newfound faith with others. Most end up overwhelming a few family members, friends, or coworkers with their zeal. Unfortunately, they often end up in arguments and some quickly grow wary of trying to share their faith. But a persistent tendency toward impetuousness will cause some to learn (usually the hard way) what does and doesn't work. If they'll hang in there long enough to temper their zeal with some good judgment, they can refine their skills at presenting the gospel.

If you are impetuous by nature, you'll have to allow God to work with you, probably for many years. Your tendency can be tamed and made useful for the Kingdom in many ways. It will begin when you recognize and admit your tendency, then start working at not running ahead of the Lord or running over your fellow human beings.

If you are not particularly impetuous by nature, you need not despair. There are plenty of areas of ministry that call for the quieter, steady individuals who move carefully and speak sparingly. Thankfully, as far as we know, Simon Peter was the only one of the disciples who was so excessively impetuous. One way of looking at it is to think it took eleven others just to balance him out! But each of those first disciples was handpicked by Jesus. Each had a role to play. And the same is true today. Each of us must come to Jesus with a "Just As I Am" attitude. "Here, Lord, take my personality, my traits and my tendencies, and mold me for your greater purpose."

"As obedient children, do not conform any longer to the evil desires you had when you lived in ignorance." (1st Peter 1:14)

c. The Call to Apostleship

READ **Matthew 10:1-4; Mark 3:13-19; Luke 6:12-16**

Jesus was making numerous disciples. Some, like the fishermen, He called directly. Others sought Him out. The multitudes enjoyed His preaching, but were becoming something of a problem in terms of logistics.

It was time for Jesus to select a specific group to which He would devote himself, preparing them through a spiritual internship for specific work in the Kingdom after He was gone. From the larger number of disciples He chose twelve. Twelve was a significant number in Jewish thinking, particularly because of the twelve tribes of Israel. Modern educators tell us a class or group of twelve is the perfect size for optimum learning as it is small enough for balanced discussion yet not so large as to let anyone feel left out.

Twelve are named. Some of them are already familiar to us. Others are practically unknown except for their mention in these lists. They are chosen for three purposes: (1) that they might be with Him, (2) that He might send them out to preach, and (3) that they have authority to drive out demons.

Don't miss the significance of the point of being with Jesus. When a replacement was chosen for Judas, the one overarching requirement was that a candidate had to have been with them during the whole time of Jesus' ministry and could thereby be a witness, with them, of His resurrection (Acts 1:21, 22). Later observers would notice the apostles had "been with Jesus" (Acts 4:13).

In their language, the word apostle meant "one sent." Our word missionary (which does not occur in Scripture) is derived from the Latin word for apostle. The role of apostle was a key one in the early church, only bestowed on a few, and not an ongoing ministry. (Except for replacing Judas at the outset, upon their deaths the apostles were not replaced.) The importance of this role is noted later in the New Testament when Paul says the church is built on the "foundation of the apostles and prophets, Jesus Christ himself being the cornerstone" (Ephesians 2:19-20). The apostles were the authoritative leaders of the early church. In addition, the Spirit gave them special gifts. Their work included preaching in sometimes hostile environments, working various miracles, writing Scripture, and planting local churches all over the known world.

Bible students can grasp something of the significance of the role of apostle, since it is mentioned as one of the areas of works in the church especially gifted by Christ (see Ephesians 4:11-16).

17

Why such a detailed explanation of the role of apostle? Because to grasp the magnitude of the role, and then consider the ones Jesus chose (especially Simon Peter!), makes one start to think in a different way about how God might look at any of us. He sees us more for what we can become, instead of just what we've been.

At one point in Simon Peter's life, if someone had told him he would spend the second half of his life as a "missionary," he would have probably laughed out loud. What about you? Have you ever perceived yourself as presently being or someday becoming a missionary? You might be closer to that role than you think!

I have been considered a missionary in two ways. First, I've gone on a number of short mission trips, both inside and outside the United States. Then I have also worked in new or small congregations in less evangelized areas of the United States, receiving support from larger, more established congregations as their "domestic missionary." You may or may not have such opportunities. If you do, be thankful, and serve as faithfully as you can. But there's a third way in which you and I and every Christian we know needs to view themselves as a missionary.

Are missionaries only those who go to distant lands, or somewhere in this country where the church is not strong, and work full-time for the church? Not if you think the "great commission" applies to all Christians (see Matthew 28:19-20; Mark 16:15-16). Your work, school, community service, and recreation all take on a different dimension when you consider you are the missionary to those with whom you interact. You may have the blessing of associating mostly with people who have heard the gospel. But surely there are a few who might otherwise never have a chance to closely relate with a devoted believer except for you. This is not intended to make you feel guilty, but to open your eyes to the potential for outreach, right where you are (read John 3:35-38).

"Peter, an apostle of Christ Jesus, To God's elect, strangers in the world, scattered . . . ." (1st Peter 1:1)

d. Natural Leadership Gets Recognized

READ **Matthew 10:1-4; Mark 3:13-19; Luke 6:12-16; Acts 1:13**

These are the lists of the apostles, recorded both in the Gospels and in the book of Acts. They were written 25-35 years after Jesus went back to Heaven. One can't help but notice Simon Peter is mentioned first in each list. This does not mean necessarily Simon Peter was a better man than the other apostles. But the story you see unfolding clearly reveals he was perceived both at the moment, as well as by history, as the unofficial leader of the apostles. Scripture does not record an instance where Jesus designated Simon Peter as the chief apostle, although the Christ may have foreseen this inevitability. It seems to have been a more natural development, especially given Simon Peter's tendency to interject himself right into the very middle of just about every situation. His natural leadership could not be overlooked or suppressed.

Let's face it – some people are just natural leaders. When they speak, people listen, respond, and follow. This does not mean they are always right or will always lead in a productive way. World history and our own experiences have shown us many natural leaders who ended up being personal disasters, causing great harm to many others. When a person senses or is told repeatedly that he or she is a natural leader, instead of having a massive ego attack, they should feel a great sense of responsibility.

Others who want or try to be leaders without having that elusive natural gift of leadership usually only frustrate themselves and those around them. It is sometimes a bitter pill to swallow to see a friend or peer being accepted as a leader when you're not. But it is at this point that dependence on the Lord is essential. Great growth and maturing can occur in the face of such realizations.

Tragically, we have seen some in the church lose their faith over this very issue. Instead of humbly accepting their non-leadership role, they have grown jealous and bitter towards those God has blessed in this way. Left unchecked, these attitudes will spoil the faith of those who hold them and negatively affect those around them (see James 3:13-16.)

Let's go back for just a moment to the idea of responsibility by one who is deemed a leader. The worldly, immature concept of leadership centers on issues like importance, power, and control. The godly response to leadership is an overwhelming sense of humility. If someone selfishly craves a leadership position, they're headed for disaster. If someone humbly accepts leadership (and all the responsibilities that go with it), they have a good chance of succeeding. They will succeed, that is, if they lean constantly on God for wisdom, strength, and courage.

I personally think there are even degrees of leadership ability among groups of leaders like we have in the church. I don't think I am necessarily the strongest or best leader in the congregation where I serve. I am frequently aware that some of my fellow leaders seem to have more of that innate sense of leadership than I do. All of the apostles were going to be called upon to be leaders, but Simon Peter seems to have ended up being at the forefront of that group. Very prayerfully and carefully you'll have to figure out if you are a leader at all, and, if so, what degree of leadership you can handle.

Whether or not we have the specific gift the Bible calls leadership (see Romans 12:8), the fact remains that sooner or later most who serve Christ for very long find themselves in situations where they have to step up and lead, and if not in a traditional or typical leadership role, at least by example.

Related to leadership is the idea of potential. Potential is obviously a great thing to have, but it can also be a heavy burden to bear! If someone thinks you have potential and you don't live up to it, then you are (perhaps very unfairly) deemed as something of a failure. While I think we should have high goals for ourselves, we would probably be better off to not listen to others talk about our potential. Likewise, I think we should take great care when talking about the potential of others, especially in the Lord's work. We should leave the foreseeing and completing to the Lord!

Because of my own above-average height, in about the 8th grade I started hearing coaches and others talk about my potential as a basketball player. At first this was exciting, but frankly, I got tired of hearing about it. It worked out for me, as I had a satisfying basketball career in high school and college. But I saw others crack under the burden of undue expectations put on them by their parents or coaches. My experience taught me that at best the whole matter of potential is very tricky!

I think in the church we may do some an injustice by too quickly dubbing them as a potential leader. And if you think, or if others have said, "you have potential" in some area (for example, preaching), take it slowly! God doesn't expect you to be exceptional overnight, even in an area where He has "gifted" you. If God wants you to do something, you'll have the time you need to discern it and develop it before you have to do it.

Don't seek to be a leader! If it's God will for you, He will let you know through those around you. Save yourself a lot of grief by committing to be, to the best of your ability, a servant. This is Christ-like! And while leaders in the church should always be "servant leaders," there's a world of need for servant non-leaders as well.

"Not because you must, but because you are willing, as God wants you to be; not greedy for money, but eager to serve; not lording it over those entrusted to you, but being examples." (1st Peter 5:2-3)

PRINCIPLE THREE

"Recognize the Pivotal Moments in Your Life"

a. The Walk He Never Forgot

READ **Matthew 14:22-36**

If you ask most people "How many humans have ever walked on water?" they would immediately answer, "Only one, Jesus." Now if you had asked how many had successfully walked on water that would be the correct answer. Of course, when we think about it, we know a second person, our beloved Simon Peter, took a brief stroll upon the waves, but with a dismal (and drenching) conclusion.

The story of Jesus' walking on the water to meet and assist his forlorn disciples in the boat is told in the books of Matthew, Mark, and John. But only Matthew gives us the additional insight into Simon Peter's participation. (If, as many believe, the book of Mark was dictated directly from Simon Peter to Mark, he may have conveniently not mentioned this most embarrassing side-story.)

Jesus' walking on the water is one of the most incredible, eye-popping miracles recorded in the New Testament. Surely only God in the flesh could accomplish such an unimaginable feat! But even more impressive is the fact that Jesus enabled Simon Peter to do the same thing! That is, until he took his eyes off of the Lord and began to fear the wind and the waves. The spiritual lessons are obvious. Keep your eyes on Christ and successfully do his bidding (even unimaginable things) without fear. Take your eyes off of Christ and look at the dangers lurking about and you're sure to fail!

There's a second important lesson, very subtly tucked in around the sinking of Simon Peter, and that is the compassion of Jesus and His willingness to rescue the faithless disciple. (It's a good thing God has His nature and not ours! In disgust, some of us might have let Simon Peter sink!)

Simon Peter is, in rapid succession, both hero and goat in this story. To his credit, he is the one willing to walk out to Jesus. Very commendable indeed, since such a feat obviously defied all the laws of nature. But then almost in the same moment, his fears overcome his faith and he starts to sink. Does this remind you of anyone you know, like yourself, perhaps?

This story becomes more meaningful when we remember Simon Peter was a fisherman. He had, no doubt, been thrown overboard a time or two in his fishing career. And we know from another gospel story he was a strong swimmer (John 21). But somehow in this situation, perhaps because of the severity of the sea, he panicked. It's like some of us who are used to fending for ourselves, but then we suddenly realize we're in over our heads in a spiritual crisis.

We have two choices: keep going on our own and perish, or call out to the Lord "Save me!"

All new Christians need to hear and take to heart a lesson something like what I call "Inevitability 101." (And older Christians need a refresher course pretty often!) All who follow Christ will, invariably, at some point take their eyes off of Jesus, and quickly begin to sink back into their former life. If we are not prepared for this certain stumble, we are sitting ducks for the Devil's playing on our sense of guilt and confusion. Did you know the word "Satan" means "the accuser?" One of his most effective ways of winning back those who converted to Christ is to accuse them with feelings like "I know I couldn't be good enough to be a Christian," or "There's just no use in my trying to be righteous."

Fortunately for the sinking Simon Peter, Jesus was close at hand to respond to his pleas for help. What makes you think He is any less interested in helping you when you stumble? Jesus didn't pay the price at Calvary for us to be almost instantly swept back into the kingdom of darkness. Never forget the lessons we learn from both the Master and the disciple in this dramatic event.

Just for fun, let me tell the story again with a little "editorial license" at the end. (This is like the disclaimer you see before many made-for-TV movies: BASED ON A TRUE STORY. That means the writers have taken great liberties with some actual events!)

The other apostles must have, at times, grown weary of Simon Peter always speaking up and acting first. Nonetheless, they admired and loved the chap. What a surprise when he bounded over the side of the boat to walk toward Jesus. They sat awestruck as he actually did it. Suddenly they were horror-struck as he began to sink. Then there was a sense of relief as Jesus plucked him from the sea. Finally, they had a case of the giggling fits (you know – that snickering you try to hide by putting your hand over your nose and mouth while your whole body is shaking.) It was quiet as Simon Peter, with Jesus' assistance, slinked back into the boat and to his seat, looking like a drowned rat! As they journeyed on, Thomas (he of "doubting Thomas" fame) asked Simon Peter in hushed tones, so as not to be heard by the Master, "So, Peter, how was the water?"

No, you won't find these details in the Bible or any reputable commentary. It's just the way I imagine it, based upon my other observations of Simon Peter and how human the other apostles had to be.

The trick to successfully enduring one of these spiritual stumbles is to remember that Jesus is close at hand and always willing to lift us up again. The world has a mindset regarding success.

Do it your way, with your strength. Be an original, be unique, and pull yourself up by your own bootstraps. Set your goals and have your dream. This approach may work in a number of areas, all except one – your spiritual life. As much as there is to love about America, this element of the American way is basically in conflict with how God wants us to be in our spiritual walk. While God gives us lots of freedom to be ourselves, He still wants us to walk in His way, with the direction and helps He provides.

"Humble yourselves, therefore, under God's mighty hand, that he may lift you up in due time." (1st Peter 5:6)

b. Don't You Guys 'Get It' Yet!

READ **Matthew 15:15,16**

How patient Jesus must have been with all of the disciples, but especially Simon Peter! On this occasion, it might seem that Jesus lost His patience with the disciples when He responded to Simon Peter's question with "Are you still so dull?"

The situation that prompts this particular incident is the telling of a parable. Some time earlier Jesus had started using parables as one of His main methods of teaching. The first time He ever taught a parable in the disciples' presence, He gave them a private explanation of not only what the parable meant, but also why parables were used. So Jesus may have known that Simon Peter's question revealed some inattention, either past or present.

It is more than fascinating to track Jesus' various reactions to the disciples. Sometimes He shows almost unbelievable patience with them. At other times He seems quick to correct, even rebuke them. In faith we'll have to accept that as the Master, He knew what He was doing with them and in each instance knew what would be in their best interest.

Some have a fanciful notion of God. They see Him as some kind of celestial grandfather who would never look disparagingly on any human misdeeds. This is, at best, wishful thinking by those who do not want to be held accountable for their actions, no matter how inappropriate. These same folks would reject the idea that God the Father or Jesus (God in the flesh) could ever lose their patience with any of us, no matter what. They are the same ones who cling to the man-made idea "A loving God could never send anyone to Hell."

Those who consider God in this way need to do some basic Bible study on God's dealings with mankind since the beginning. God set the rules in the Garden of Eden. When they were broken, punishment followed, but not without the promise of eventual redemption. Later God repented (regretted) He had made mankind, and considered totally obliterating humans. God caused a worldwide flood, which destroyed many wicked people, and mankind had a new beginning through eight persons. But the rainbow was, and is, God's reminder that He would never destroy mankind in this way again. Throughout the entirety of the Old Testament, we have story after story of God's disciplining people who disobeyed His Will. But with the discipline there was always the underlying principle of His great love and desire for a covenant relationship with His created beings.

That great love sent Jesus to the world and allowed him to suffer the punishment we deserve.

An instance here or there of Jesus becoming a bit beleaguered with the slowness of his disciples' comprehension is not reason for us to doubt that He was the Christ. On the contrary, He had every right to question their openness and to challenge them to be better learners. In the light of numerous occasions of His having to forgive them, an occasional upbraiding is not an indication of lack or love or His genuine concern that they learn to do better.

Popular at the moment in our American speech is the phrase "You just don't get it!" This is usually said in derision. But it can also be said as an impassioned appeal for someone to pay closer attention – to think about what they are missing. We have no reason to believe Jesus wanted to hurt his disciples, but, on the contrary, wanted them to grasp fully his teachings and their import.

All teachers encourage their students to ask questions. Young scholars are implored with "There's no such thing as a bad question!" Yet every teacher occasionally has one of those students who, in the face of detailed explanation after detailed explanation, will show an incredible knack of asking a question that indicates they weren't paying attention at all. (Impetuous kids nearly drive teachers crazy.) Jesus' question "Are you still so dull?" must have been asked on such an occasion.

Jesus was trying to get His disciples to learn to take His teachings and then think for themselves. A teacher who can get his or her students to think is a teacher par excellence! Christians must learn to think for themselves beyond the sermons and classes they hear. There is simply not enough time in anyone's schedule for a person to hear the answers to every single question with which they'll have to deal. Good hearers will have to learn to be good thinkers.

You know how they say your own offspring will punish you for the way you were when you were a child? I think the same is true for those of us who were simultaneously impetuous and inattentive as students and now try to teach others. I cannot believe the questions I am sometimes asked after teaching or preaching! I am sometimes flabbergasted that I could be so misunderstood or not understood at all. But at the same time, this can work to sharpen those of us who preach and teach. Serious teachers learn that to a large extent they can avoid some of these problems through more thorough preparation. The possibility of being misunderstood should always make spiritual teachers more deliberate in their presentations. But with all of that, none of us is going to be a better teacher than Jesus was. Someone will be eager to ask a question proving he or she hasn't been paying attention at all! Such occasions cause a teacher to pray for patience and a gentle spirit.

No one who's serious about his or her faith wants to get to the judgment scene and hear Jesus say, in effect, "You just didn't get it, did you?" According to the Lord's own words, some are going to be shocked and saddened, even in spite of their religious activity, when they hear "Depart from me; I never knew you" (Matthew 7:27).

"Therefore, prepare your minds for action; be self-controlled; set your hope fully on the grace to be given you when Jesus Christ is revealed." (1st Peter 1:13)

c. The Great Confession

READ **Matthew 16:13-20; Mark 8:29; Luke 9:20**

This is one of those pivotal moments in the ministry of Jesus and in the life of Simon Peter as well. The apostles had returned from a preaching journey. Jesus wanted to hear their report as to what people were saying about Him. There were some interesting answers. And then suddenly He turns the question directly back to the apostles: "But who do you say that I am?"

There must have been a moment of stunned silence. We shouldn't be surprised at who speaks up with the answer. And what an answer it was! In fact, it may have been the greatest answer ever given to such a profound question. But before we look at the answer itself, let's not miss the point that this question has been raised millions of times since that fateful day. Each person who hears the message of Christ must, at some point, make a decision as to what he or she thinks of Jesus. Who is He, really?

Angels had announced to shepherds that the baby they would find lying in a manger was "Christ the Lord" (Luke 2:11). Eight days later in the temple the aged Simeon recognized baby Jesus as the Christ. John the Baptist seemingly alluded to the nearness of the Christ during His ministry. Andrew, Simon Peter's brother, had boldly declared, "We have found the Messiah!" (See John 1:41). The idea of Jesus being the long-awaited Messiah ("Christ" in Greek) had, no doubt, crossed the minds of the apostles many times. They had witnessed many discussions regarding His true identity. Plus they had heard Him teach and seen Him perform many miracles. But Jesus Himself, as far as we know, had not asked anyone a question regarding His true identity in such a direct way.

And now the moment of truth comes and Simon Peter boldly declares, "You are the Christ (Messiah), the Son of the living God!" One can't help but wonder if after he said it, Simon Peter might have had a surprised look on his face like, "Did I say that?"

Jesus immediately commends the outspoken apostle and points out this realization did not come from "flesh and blood," that is, it was not deduced from human thinking (or reasoning). Humans are unable within themselves to grasp the plan of God. It must be revealed unto them. This kind of understanding has to come from God.

Does this mean God miraculously put the thought into Simon Peter's mind and the words into his mouth? No! It means God had been working through what had been seen and heard by all the apostles to convince them that Jesus really was the Messiah. God will not make any of us believe; it's a decision we must make for ourselves. But God has made it possible through countless evidences and the power of the gospel itself for us to believe.

After considering this breakthrough moment for Simon Peter, I'm reminded of the well-known words of a beloved hymn: "How precious did that grace appear, the hour I first believed!" Do you remember the first time it all clicked for you in your thinking and you suddenly grasped the message of the gospel in a much deeper way than ever before? Actually, I can remember a number of times when I have suddenly, often unexpectedly, moved to a new level of faith and understanding. It is, to say the least, exhilarating! Remembering such moments makes it easier for me to keep on seeking new insights. And I'm not worried – no matter how much I grow or learn, the possibility for further spiritual awakening is infinite!

Have you made the good confession of your faith in Jesus as the Son of God? (See Matthew 10:31-32; Romans 10:9-10; Hebrews 4:14.) Confession of one's faith is a precursor to baptism (Acts 8:37-39). Read Acts 8:37-39 if you can from the King James or New King James Versions. Some other versions relegate verse 37 to the footnotes, which seems unfortunate.

"Always be prepared to give an answer to everyone who asks you to give the reason for the hope that you have." (1st Peter 2:15)

d. A Rock and the Rock

Jesus continues His response to Simon Peter's dramatic confession. And He finally gives us some insight as to why He nicknamed Simon "rock" (Peter, Cephas) so many months before. A careful look at the text shows Jesus actually describing two different kinds of rocks. Only Matthew records this intriguing dialogue between Jesus and Simon Peter. Jesus was, no doubt, speaking in Aramaic, the language of that region. But the New Testament writers wrote in Greek, the literary language understood throughout the world at that time. It is the Greek text which shows a distinction between the two kinds of stone. Jesus says "You are Peter" and the Greek word Petros means a small stone, the kind you can skip across the water. He then says "Upon this rock" and here He used the Greek word Petra, which refers to a large piece of bedrock (for our imaginations, something like the Rock of Gibraltar).

The nickname Jesus had given Simon was complimentary. It indicated strength and stability. (Athletes and movie stars have been given nicknames like Rock or Rocky to tout their toughness or tenacity.) But in comparison to the truth Simon Peter has just confessed, the apostle himself is a relatively small stone.

As one analyzes this passage, it becomes abundantly clear Jesus is using a play on words to distinguish between that upon which His church would be built and that with which it would be built: you obviously build on a solid foundation with smaller bits of material.

Jesus' identity as the Christ is the foundation upon which the Lord will build His church. The apostle Paul says "For no one can lay any foundation other than the one already laid, which is Jesus Christ" (1 Corinthians 3:11). Later, Simon Peter himself would write about the church being made of "living stones" (Christians), but with Jesus Himself as the only "cornerstone" (1 Peter 2:4-8).

Some have erroneously concluded Jesus promised to build the church upon the man Simon Peter. This is entirely inconsistent with the whole of Scripture. Jesus is the only one qualified to be Savior, Lord, King, High Priest, Head of the church, and Cornerstone.

There's a tendency among some religious people to refer to the congregation they attend as "my church" or "our church." This can be innocent enough if simply referring to where they invest themselves in the worship and service of the Lord. However, some presume to actually have "their church." They think it belongs to them and they can do with it what they want, doctrinally, legally, etc.

Unfortunate also is the tendency some have to refer to a particular congregation by the preacher who labors there as "Brother So-and-so's church." In the face of these tendencies, we need to remember who purchased the church with His own blood (Acts 20:28) and who is the head of it (Ephesians 2:17; Colossians 3:18). Remember what Jesus said in the passage upon which this chapter is based: "I will build MY CHURCH" (Matthew 16:18, emphasis mine, KSH).

With some input from my good friend Don Garrett, I developed a sermon I call "Whose Church Is It, Anyway?" The main point of the sermon is that ownership, direction, and purpose of the body of Christ, and any local assembly of it, belong to God. In the few times I've given this sermon, I usually say something like "It's not Keith's church, it's not the leadership's church, it's not the members' church, and it's not some special group's church. It's God's church, and we're all just small parts of it. Our task is to humbly figure out where and how God wants us to fit in."

Jesus has been building his church for nearly 2,000 years and the building of it continues to this day. And He's not building it with literal bricks and mortar or any other earthly material – He's building it with people!

Technically, no one ever joins the Lord's church. When a person becomes a Christian, he or she is added to the church by the Lord (Acts 2:47). Simon Peter was a stone in the building plans, an important part of the foundation (Ephesians 2:17), but not the cornerstone. Jesus adequately fills that place. Have you found your place in the church Jesus is building? It will be most helpful to see yourself as one of those living stones in the hands of the master builder.

"As you come to him, the living Stone – rejected by men but chosen by God and precious to him – you also, like living stones, are being built into a spiritual house to be a holy priesthood, offering spiritual sacrifices acceptable to God through Jesus Christ." (1st Peter 2:2, 5)

PRINCIPLE FOUR

"With Grace Comes Responsibility"

a. Here Are the Keys

READ **Matthew 16:19**

You've probably heard dozens of them, those corny jokes about one or more souls reaching Heaven, knocking on the "pearly gates," and being met by "Saint Peter." And why does Simon Peter greet them? It's because, as the reasoning goes, he was given the "keys to the kingdom of heaven." No matter how much you enjoy the jokes, this is almost certainly not the way anyone will enter Heaven. But that's a different Bible study!

Just after Simon Peter's dramatic confession of the true identity of Jesus, the Lord said an amazing thing. "I will give you the keys of the kingdom of heaven, and whatever you bind on earth shall be bound in heaven, and whatever you loose on earth shall be loosed in heaven." What could that possibly mean? First, although Jesus is responding to the statement by Simon Peter, there's reason to strongly suspect that this part of the address is given to all of the apostles. Still, it was Simon Peter who first preached the gospel to the Jews on the Day of Pentcost (Acts 2). And it was also Simon Peter who first presented the gospel to a completely Gentile audience (Acts 10). But a broader look at the work of the apostles, as well as the first-century prophets, shows their teachings and writings "bound" and "loosed" the doctrine of the church, then and ever since.

Jesus once described himself as "the door" through which the sheep would have to enter to have abundant life (John 10). Wouldn't one who shares the gospel with others, be they an apostle of the first-century or a Christian of any century, be using those "keys of the kingdom?" Incredible as it is to imagine, Jesus has entrusted his disciples (past and present) to show others the way to the "door" and how to enter through it.

One summer between years of college, I was privileged to go on a 3-week evangelistic trip to Geneva, Switzerland. Veteran missionary Stanley Shipp led the effort. Stanley and I would become dear friends, working together on many other trips and projects, and on the same ministerial staff in St. Louis. But at the outset of this trip we barely knew each other. When we arrived in Geneva, Stanley went about the business of dividing the 100+ workers into teams of eight, each with a guy designated as leader. Most of these leaders were high school boys from the Abilene, Texas, youth group where Stanley was a minister. I was passed over in the assignments. To be honest, I felt it was a little strange that boys younger than me had

34

been given such key roles, but just figured it was because Stanley didn't know me. However, later in the day Stanley called me aside and said, "I want to give you the keys." I said "What keys?" And he said "The keys to the outer and inner doors of the YMCA where all you guys are staying. Since you will be getting back there each evening after they close, someone will have to be able to get all of you in." Surprisingly, I had been suddenly promoted from an unknown guy to most of the workers to a terribly important position (especially to the male campaigners at about eleven o'clock each evening!), all because I had the keys! I was both honored and humbled in the same moment, and worked hard at faithfully executing my task each night while we were in Geneva.

Do you ever stop and think when someone hands you the keys to their car what a significant thing it is? They own the car, but they are entrusting it, for a little while, to you. How much more significant for Jesus to turn the keys of is Kingdom over to any of us! You may not be a well-known preacher, a popular author, or even feel particularly appreciated in your local church. But if you understand the gospel, you should appreciate the fact that Jesus has given you "the keys to the Kingdom," just as he did Simon Peter and the other apostles. Humbly accept your task and faithfully pursue your assignment.

"But just as he who called you is holy, so be holy in all you do, for it is written 'Be holy, because I am holy'." (1st Peter 1:15, 16)

b. The Rebuker Becomes the Rebukee

READ **Matthew 16:21-23**

The hearts of the apostles, and especially Simon Peter's, must have been soaring! He has just heard Jesus say to him, "Blessed are you, Simon son of John." All of them have heard the incredible truths being discussed. The promise of the "keys of the kingdom" probably has their imaginations running wild. Then the other shoe drops!

From that time on, Jesus begins to plainly describe the dramatic events ahead, including His suffering, death, and resurrection. This is just a little bit too much reality for our impetuous friend Simon Peter. He may have been thinking, "Oh, come on! Let's enjoy a little more of this Messiah talk." And clearly he was taken aback by the details of Jesus' approaching death. This seemed unthinkable! He'll just straighten out Jesus' thinking on this little matter right away. In a private conversation with Jesus, Simon Peter begins to rebuke the Lord.

Rebuke is a strong word. Several versions and the original language have been checked. They all say rebuke. We may be wishing for Simon Peter's sake that he would have "inquired" or perhaps "expressed concern." But no! Our man, no doubt feeling pretty full of himself with his fresh commendation, takes it upon himself to rebuke the Son of God!

It's important to not merely interpret Jesus' response as one of anger at being rebuked. Several times in the Old Testament God had shown remarkable patience with godly men who more or less argued with Him in prayer. Jesus has shown this same kind of patience throughout His ministry, answering both questioners and accusers. No, it's not just Simon Peter's impetuous nature that bothered the Lord (although the apostle was out of line!). It's Simon Peter challenging the very plan to fulfill Jesus' mission, which must happen exactly as described. This is the lesson that must be impressed upon Simon Peter and the others.

And the rebuke Jesus gives back to Simon Peter is a zinger for sure! In fact, it's a compound zinger. He calls him Satan. Ouch! He says in effect "Get out of my way!" or "Get out of my sight!" He says the apostle is a stumbling block (hindrance or distraction) to Him. He says Simon Peter does not have in mind the things of God, but the things of men. Wow!

Has it ever occurred to you in studying this passage that Jesus makes use of a third type of stone, the "stumbling block?" Notice

36

particularly how Jesus says Simon Peter does not have in mind the things of God because he is thinking like "men," that is, from a human perspective. He was commended earlier because he did not learn the great things he said about Jesus from any man. There's a simple but profound challenge herein for all who are serious about serving the Lord. We must constantly be aligning our thoughts with God, from His Word. We are not to depend or rely just upon how we were brought up, or ride the coattails of someone else's faith, or any conclusions we've come to on our own. In other words, we must rely upon the one authoritative source of truth we have at our disposal – the Word of God – and not on any of the other sources we are accustomed to trusting, including our own feelings.

Many, if rebuked this severely, would have gotten in a huff and stopped following Jesus. (Sadly, we've seen some depart from Christianity over much less – but not Simon Peter!) Oh, we can be sure it stung him a bit. But he didn't quit. Simon Peter had that which most of us need in greater abundance – steadfastness.

I've learned the hard way, just as you have, that speaking to someone in (sinful) anger, even if seemingly justified, usually does more harm than good. Learning the Biblical injunction "In your anger do not sin" (Ephesians 4:26) is a challenge for all. Also, like all church leaders, I've had the difficult task of having to rebuke some erring Christian. Not fun at all! But in both moments of inappropriate anger or necessary rebuking, there's one mistake I haven't made – using the words Jesus used to rebuke Simon Peter that is, calling him "Satan." I don't know how I came to be so convinced of this. But somewhere along the way I became aware that only the Lord could say these things in this way to one of his followers. None of us has the position, authority, or wisdom to make such a rebuke. Jesus knew Simon Peter well enough to know what He could and couldn't say. And Jesus could also do something we can't: He could look into Simon Peter's heart and mind and discern his motives. We can't do that. We shouldn't try.

Don't try to outthink God! Question him – maybe? Flat out disagree with His Word, never! If while determined to be a disciple of Jesus you find yourself resisting the Word of God, it's time to ask yourself if you "have in mind the things of God" or "the things of men."

Proverbs 15:31 says, "He who listens to a life-giving rebuke will be at home among the wise." One way to prepare for the awkward task of rebuking others is to learn how to receive a rebuke yourself. Although it is always difficult, in order to be a growing disciple one must learn to take heed to rebukes not only from personal Bible reading, and Biblical preaching and teaching, but also godly peers.

"Whoever would love life and see good days must keep his tongue from evil and his lips from deceitful speech. He must turn from evil and do good; he must seek peace and pursue it. For the eyes of the Lord are on the righteous and his ears are attentive to their prayer, but the face of the Lord is against those who do evil." (1st Peter 3:10-12; Psalm 34:12-16)

c. The Inner Circle

READ **Matthew 17:1-13; Mark 9:2-13; Luke 9:37-43**

The twelve apostles spent a great deal of time with Jesus, hearing him teach and seeing him perform miracles. But on several special occasions Jesus takes three of the apostles – Simon Peter, James, and John – to share in an even more personal form of training.

One of the most memorable of these events with the "inner circle" is the transfiguration. As best we can determine nothing like it has ever happened before or since. It was glorious, as you can read in the details. It was, in effect, a multiple miracle.

But before we look at this incredible event, let's not miss a subtle but important point regarding Jesus' discipling of Simon Peter. We leave Matthew chapter 16 with the words of Jesus' stinging rebuke of the apostle. Although six days pass, as chapter 17 unfolds we see Jesus taking "Peter, James and John" with him to another special event. With all that transpired between Jesus and the apostle in that earlier conversation, it did not alter Jesus' determination to continue his personal training of Simon Peter. How many times have you seen or heard of situations where after there were "words" between a person of greater authority and one of his or her subordinates, the one in authority has punished the subordinate through a period of censure or even neglect? Not so here between Jesus and Simon Peter!

The first part of the transfiguration was the dramatic change in Jesus' appearance. His face "shone like the sun" and his clothes "became as white as light." (If you remember the Bible's several references to God's living in resplendent light, and in fact being the essence of light, then you realize this event is actually an earthly view of Jesus' heavenly appearance.)

The second part of the miracle was equally sensational. To help make the point about the supremacy of Jesus, God the Father summons forth Moses (the Lawgiver, and the greatest hero of the Old Testament) and Elijah (the fiery prophet who was unrivaled for his courage and forthrightness for God) from the dead. They appear! Imagine how overwhelmed these apostles must have been. Great spiritual heroes, who had lived and died centuries before, suddenly appeared. Imagine their delight but also their bewilderment at seeing such an occurrence.

But let's go back for a moment to the issue of Jesus' so-called "inner circle." Some people are not comfortable with the thought of Jesus having some friends or associates closer to him than others.

They think He should have somehow shared the same level of relationship with every human being with whom He dealt. This is unrealistic as well as unfair. While we sometimes struggle to accept Jesus' divinity, we must also strive to accept His humanity. He had several circles of friends – some closer, some not so close.

Try to imagine a target like you'd use in archery – a series of circles each successively larger, moving away from a central point. In your mind, let each circle represent a level of friendship (personal relationship) with Jesus. So the first circle would be the Apostle John, apparently His closest friend. Next would be the inner circle of Simon Peter, James, and John. Then there were the rest of the twelve apostles. Next would be the large band of disciples who frequently accompanied Jesus on His travels. Then there were the multitudes that listened to his teaching and sought various miracles. Finally there's the rest of the world, from which people can be attracted as seekers, and then perhaps become disciples.

I've been privileged to be in a few of these "inner circles" of leadership while serving on church staffs, boards of directors, and in an eldership. Selection to such positions can be very flattering. But as many of you know, there's a lot more to it than prestige, real or imagined. With such positions come responsibility, accountability, and sometimes vulnerability.

Some people, like Simon Peter and James and John, will by their very natures or circumstances always be thrust into positions of leadership. Others, like the nine rarely mentioned apostles, can have important roles without being at the very "hub" of everything. The latter realm is where most Christians function best. Each of us must realistically assess our strengths and weaknesses and thereby determine where we can most effectively serve.

As kids on the playground we all learned the simple truth about too many chiefs and not enough Indians. Churches don't function as well as they should when the wrong people try to be the chiefs or when everyone thinks they should be one of the chiefs.

In recent years much has been said about having a personal relationship with Jesus. Every serious disciple should strive to know Jesus as well as possible by reading and listening over and over to His story. Also a vital part of the story is the realization that God, Jesus, and the Holy Spirit are aware of and concerned about each of us as individuals. Hymns that speak of the friendship between the Lord and us are comforting and encouraging. It is natural to grow so much in your admiration and faith that you'll boldly say "Jesus is my best friend!"

Being realistic though, we recognize we weren't there as one of the "inner circle," or one on the twelve, or even in the throngs who heard him preach. By faith, and only in our imaginations, do we know what Jesus looked like, or the tone of his voice, or some of his personal mannerisms. He won't make a special appearance to us or visit our bedside in this realm. Not until He makes his triumphant return to take us to Heaven will we "see him as he is" (1st John 3:2). Until then, in faith we will continue to grow in our relationship with him based upon what we can know of him from the Scriptures.

"We did not follow cleverly invented stories when we told you about the power and coming of our Lord Jesus Christ, but we were eyewitnesses of his majesty." (2nd Peter 1:16)

d. Count on Simon Peter to Say Something

READ **Matthew 17:4; Mark 9:5; Luke 9:33**

Impetuous people, like Simon Peter, have a knack for stating the obvious. Oh, they don't intend to be trite or ridiculous. They just have a compulsion to speak, even if it's not particularly edifying to those around them.

The three apostles have just witnessed one of the most spectacular events of all time, beyond their imagination, because nothing like it had ever happened before. This calls for someone to say something profound, a quote for the ages. What does Simon Peter say? (Are you ready for this?) "Lord, it is good for us to be here."

Luke's account does offer, "He did not know what he was saying." Also, only Luke records that "Peter and his companions were very sleepy," but were awoken fully when they saw Christ's glory and the two other men. Maybe Simon Peter was not being so impetuous, but was speaking in that confused state of mind that we sometimes experience after being suddenly woken up.

Now in Simon Peter's defense, he is not shy about speaking up. The other apostles always knew, even without having Jesus' powers of discernment, where Simon Peter stood. And you can further appreciate the fact his heart was usually in the right place, even if his comprehension of the matter was limited. Such is the case with the remainder of Simon Peter's response.

Simon Peter suggests he or they build three shelters (shrines, altars, or monuments) to the three spiritual giants who have just appeared – Moses, Elijah, and Jesus. On the face of it, this is a noble suggestion. The apostle is giving more credit to Jesus than most would, equating Him with these Old Testament heroes. But at the same time Simon Peter is forgetting the full implication of the momentous confession he himself had made just days before. "You are the Christ (Messiah), the Son of the Living God!" Perhaps Simon Peter's impetuousness didn't allow him enough time to think it through. The Messiah is not equal to but much greater than even these legendary characters.

God the Father himself quickly intercedes with a booming pronouncement. For even as Simon Peter spoke, a cloud enveloped them and God said "This is my son; listen to him!" God dramatically stated Jesus' pre-eminence over all, including Moses the law-giver and Elijah, foremost of the prophets. This terrified the three apostles, and they fell to the ground in reverence and fear. Jesus touched them and reassured them and told them to "get up." After warning them not to tell what they've seen, they headed down the mountain to return to more normal discipleship.

Think about it. All of the apostles are seeing and hearing unbelievable things on a daily basis. These three have privately witnessed this spectacular occurrence. And now they are in even more rarefied company, for they have heard the voice of God! This is not lost on Simon Peter. This event is the only one from Jesus' ministry he specifically cites in his writings (see 2 Peter 1:16-18).

Have you ever wondered what the voice of God sounds like? I try to imagine it might be like a combination of all the best radio announcers I've ever heard – rich and deep and clear. When depicted in movies God's voice often has a thunderous ring to it. Or it might not be spectacular at all. Remember, God sometimes reveals himself in things that might seem rather ordinary. Even Jesus, God in the flesh, was not particularly striking or handsome (Isaiah 53:2b).

I have no reason to expect to hear the actual voice of God until I get to Heaven. But I want to be listening for that voice indirectly, in the wind, in the babbling brook, in children's laughter, in the bird's song, and in my own voice as I speak to the hurting or grieving in a godly way.

Elijah heard "that still small voice," which some think was God whispering, but others interpret as God speaking to the prophet at a deep inner (spiritual) level. It excites me to "hear" God's voice resonating in my mind and heart every time I honestly read His Word or listen to it being preached. That is enough for now.

If you haven't done so already, try to develop sensitivity to hear and see God and Jesus in your imagination. You will do so knowing it is, at best, a speculation that falls short of the glory you'll behold when you actually see them face-to-face. Your mental picture of the Father and the Son will gradually change as you learn more about them from the Word. And eventually you may not even conceive them as an image (physical characteristics), but more as a concept (spiritual characteristics).

"For he received honor and glory from God the Father when the voice came to him from the Majestic Glory, saying, 'This is my son, whom I love; with him I am well pleased.' We ourselves heard this voice that came from heaven when we were with him on the sacred mountain." (2nd Peter 1:17-18)

PRINCIPLE FIVE

"There's No Substitute For On The Job Training"

a. Where Else Could We Go?

READ **John 6:66-71**

This is one of the most dramatic episodes in Jesus' discipling of Simon Peter. Earlier in the chapter Jesus has been teaching about "eating his flesh" and "drinking his blood." This is not, as some first-century critics asserted, any kind of endorsement of cannibalism! It may be alluding to the Lord's Supper, the memorial meal instituted by Jesus just before His death, and practiced in the church ever since. It most definitely is teaching about the seriousness and demands of having a relationship with the Christ.

For the first time in His ministry, Jesus' remarks prompt a mass exodus. People are leaving in droves, saying these are "hard teachings." Jesus turns to his disciples and asks "What about you? Are you also going to leave?"

Who else but Simon Peter gushes forth with the answer! But here's a rare occasion where he had exactly the right response, without quickly blowing it by then saying something ridiculous or wrong.

Simon Peter said (and this is rich!) "To whom could we go? You have the words of eternal life; and we have believed, and have come to know, that you the Holy One of God." Wow, Simon Peter! Right on! A+! You hit the nail right on the head! Simon Peter stumbled and fumbled a lot, but he knew deep in his heart that he and the others had found the Messiah, the genuine article. Turning back now was not an option.

This passage reminds me of two of my favorite hymns. Indulge me as I stop and sing them right now. (You may sing along if you like!)

WONDERFUL WORDS OF LIFE

Sing them over again to me, wonderful words of life,
Let me more of their beauty see, wonderful words of life.
Words of life and beauty, teach me faith and duty,
Beautiful words, wonderful words, wonderful words of life;
Beautiful words, wonderful words, wonderful words of life.

Christ, the blessed One, gives to all, wonderful words of life,
Sinner, list to the loving call, wonderful words of life.
All so freely given, wooing us to heaven;
Beautiful words, wonderful words, wonderful words of life;

Beautiful words, wonderful words, wonderful words of life.
Sweetly echo the gospel call, wonderful words of life;
Offer pardon and peace to all, wonderful words of life.
Jesus, only Savior, sanctify for ever;
Beautiful words, wonderful words, wonderful words of life;
Beautiful words, wonderful words, wonderful words of life.

WHERE COULD I GO BUT TO THE LORD (verse 1 and chorus)

Living below in this old sinful world, hardly a comfort can afford,
But when my soul needs manna from above, (now tell me)
Where could I go but to the Lord!

Where could I go, oh, where could I go?
Seeking a refuge for my soul,
Needing a friend, to save me in the end,
Where could I got but to the Lord!

Read John 6:68-69 over and over, however many times it takes, until you are overwhelmed with the splendor, the majesty, of what Simon Peter has just said. And as you obtain or retain the same mind-set of Simon Peter on the truthfulness and relevance of Jesus' words, never under any circumstance turn away from that conviction!

"And though you do not see him now, you believe in him and are filled with an inexpressible and glorious joy, for you are receiving the goal of your faith, the salvation of your souls." (1st Peter 1:8-9)

b. Put 'On the Spot' For the Master

READ Matthew 17:24-27

This has to be one of the least taught and therefore least understood episodes from the gospels, and it involves Jesus and Simon Peter. We can only guess why the tax collector approached Simon Peter. Perhaps he thought of him as one of Jesus' key people. In any case, the apostle is suddenly put on the spot, answering questions for Jesus.

One of the most unsettling positions for many Christians, especially recent converts, is to suddenly find themselves as a spokesperson for Christianity. Someone asks the new believer a tough spiritual question, and suddenly he or she feels like the bright lights have come on and the cameras are rolling. The neophyte disciple wants to answer correctly, and does his or her best to provide some kind of answer.

There's a lot about this particular incident with Simon Peter we do not know. We have no reason to think Jesus didn't pay his taxes to the civil authorities or, as in this instance, the temple tax required of free Jewish men over twenty years of age. (Perhaps the tax collector was just another of the many trying to trap Jesus in his words or actions.) When asked if his Master pays the temple tax, Simon Peter answers "Yes." Upon returning home, Jesus knew about the encounter (probably from his ability, while in human form, to still be all-knowing as God). The Lord engages Simon Peter in a brief discussion regarding the issue of taxation.

Jesus demonstrates here a rationale we see him address elsewhere (see Matthew 22:21) about paying taxes. Paul further addresses the topic of conduct toward the state in Romans chapter 13. Seeking not to offend, Jesus gives Simon Peter directions to go fishing and take a coin from the mouth of the first fish he catches. This money would satisfy both Jesus' and Simon Peter's tax obligations. This is one of the lesser-known miracles of Jesus, almost as obscure as the incident and conversation prompting it.

Getting into the business world after twenty years in church work, I finally learned some things I should have known from being a Christian. As a sales and service representative for a large company carrying literally hundreds of products, with numerous technical variations to each product, I was initially calling on customers despite my very limited product knowledge. In the first year or two I had to say dozens of times "I don't know, but I'll find out and get back to you." Most of my customers were very patient and seemed genuinely surprised when I actually followed through and got back to them with an answer. Sometimes when we Christians are put on the spot, we forget this simple practice. Maybe our pride makes us want to give an answer, even if it's wrong. Let's always strive to be honest in this regard. Those we are trying to influence for Christ will in the long run appreciate us more for it.

You've probably had one or more of those awkward situations where you were suddenly put on the spot for Jesus. When I had started my new job, the word spread quickly that a preacher (horror the thought!) was working there. After about a week, I was approached by Tony, the warehouse foreman who asked, "So, you are a preacher?" And I reservedly said, "Yes." "Well, I got a question for you" he stated. (I was just then noticing several others from the warehouse and beyond had quietly moved closer to hear the conversation.) I thought to myself, "Oh no!" He proceeded with, "Adam and Eve – did they have bellybuttons?" Fortunately I had recently heard someone joking about this same question. So I promptly replied with a straight face, "Yes – they had 'outies'!" Everyone paused for a second, then burst into laughter. I was quickly accepted on the staff, and enjoyed good relationships throughout my tenure there, especially with my (now) good friend Tony. All subsequent spiritual questions, which came up from time to time, were of a serious nature.

Read or re-read from 1 Peter 2:15 Simon Peter's practical advice about answering crucial spiritual questions. It does not say we should be prepared to answer every possible theological question, or even all the ins and outs of the plan of salvation. But it is always a worthwhile goal to learn as much doctrine as you can to be prepared to share the details if you are given the opportunity. And it doesn't hurt if you can also remember a few clever responses to frivolous questions like the one cited above! But for any believer, even if you became a Christian only yesterday, Simon Peter's admonition still holds: we should be prepared to give a reason for the hope we have within ourselves. Did you get that? The HOPE we have within ourselves. Be able to tell people why you're glad you believe – that because you've done what God has said your sins are forgiven and you're going to Heaven!

And by the way, as a part of your effective witness, so as not to offend, pay your taxes and all your other bills. Living within your means and meeting your financial obligations are a good testimony to the power of God working in your life. Being a deadbeat is not a good testimony!

"But do this with gentleness and respect, keeping a clear conscience, so that those who speak maliciously against your good behavior in Christ may be ashamed of their slander." (1st Peter 3:16)

c. Better than Most, But Not Good Enough

READ **Matthew 18:21-22**

Jesus had been privately teaching his disciples about matters of humility, seeking the wanderers, and dealing with one who has sinned against you. Simon Peter, always the inquisitive one, has a question. But with the question he poses a possible answer. Specifically, he addresses the difficult matter of how many times to forgive someone. When you stop and think about it, Simon Peter was actually quite generous with his offer of seven times.

Remember, these Jews are the original "eye for an eye, tooth for a tooth" people! Some more compassionate rabbis had suggested the possible forgiveness of a person three times. (Compare this with the difficulty some people have forgiving another person even once!)

Let's give Simon Peter the benefit of the doubt here. We don't sense any grandstanding in his question and suggested answer. Maybe he's been listening to Jesus long enough for some of the mercy to be rubbing off. But Jesus, no doubt, shocked Simon Peter and the others with his answer – seventy times seven! (Now for you literalists, this doesn't give you license to keep a running tally up to 490, and then really let somebody have it!) Jesus' words have special significance when we consider the importance Jewish people attached to the number seven. It was a perfect number, representing wholeness in every way. So seven times seven times ten (another important number) represents not the literal number 490, but infinity! In today's slang, this could be paraphrased "You forgive people, if necessary, a gazillion times."

This is one area where I'm definitely not like Simon Peter. When he offered the idea of forgiving someone seven times, that's way beyond where I've been most of my life. I'm something of a "closet resenter," if you know what I mean. When people have done me wrong, I want them to apologize, pronto! Well, as you know, that rarely happens, at least not the way you want it to. Then you end up holding a little private grudge. I struggled for years with the simple question of whether you can forgive someone who hasn't specifically asked for forgiveness. You can wrestle with that one at the theological level for a long time, but a practical solution is what most of us need.

You see, I gladly accept the fact that I've been forgiven countless times by God for my sinful actions. But I can also reason that I have repented and asked his forgiveness, both in my initial obedience to the gospel and in an ongoing way in my Christian life.

So what about those who hurt me, but never ask for my forgiveness? Since it is The Father and The Son, of course, who will ultimately judge people, all of us will be better served by leaving all of that in their capable hands. Romans 12 is a great source of encouragement in this regard, especially verses 14 and 17-21.

In the verses just prior to Simon Peter's question, Jesus states the procedure for dealing with an offense (Matthew 18:15-18). Oftentimes it works beautifully; sometimes it doesn't. Yes, people should apologize for personal offenses, and they should likewise repent (publicly if necessary) for sinful actions. But sometimes they don't. When that happens, my need is to find some way to be at peace with the situation, which ultimately will produce a greater sense of peace in me.

The only thing I've found so far that helps is to try to develop an attitude of forgiveness toward those who've trespassed against me. By this I mean I try to think about how much I would like to forgive them, or how willing I would be to forgive them if and when they ask. This may seem corny to you, but for me it often helps take the sting out of some personal hurts.

How are you doing at forgiving others, either when they ask for forgiveness, or even more importantly, when they don't? One of the toughest teachings of Jesus to accept is His making our forgiveness conditional upon our ability to forgive those who've sinned against us. That last comment will likely upset some. But if Matthew 6:14 and related passages (see below) don't say that, then what do they say? (The point here is not some legalistic "eye for an eye," but one's inability to appreciate his or her own forgiveness, as evidenced by refusing the same forgiveness to some other person.)

If you are one who finds forgiving others especially difficult, spend some time studying Matthew 6:12-14, Matthew 18:23-35, Ephesians 4:32, and Colossians 3:13. And consider also the earlier suggestion about developing an attitude of forgiveness.

"Do not repay evil with evil, or insult with insult, but with blessing, because to this you were called so that you may inherit a blessing." (1st Peter 3:9)

d. Wondering Out Loud

READ **Matthew 19:16-30; Mark 10:17-31; Luke 18:18-30**

This brief dialogue between Jesus and Simon Peter occurs immediately after the better-known conversation between Jesus and the rich young ruler. After the young man went away sorrowful, Jesus used the occasion to talk about the relationship and possible strife between riches and the kingdom of God. The disciples were astonished at what they heard. The disciples as a group ask a question about the possibility of anyone being saved. (We've all gone through those times of discovering some new understanding of the magnitude of God's commands and wondering if anybody can live up to it.) Then Simon Peter, always the prime candidate to ask probing questions, seems to wonder out loud about the future of those following the Christ.

Do you sense, perhaps, a bit of a change in Simon Peter? His nature will always have him be the one who speaks up. But maybe, just maybe, his impetuousness is slowly changing to a more sincere inquisitiveness. In effect, he's asking "What about us? What's going to become of us? What shall we have to show for our having been a part of all this?"

In all these situations where Jesus introduced profound new thinking, we have to be a bit reserved in judging Simon Peter and the others too harshly. The collective thinking of all of Christendom has had nearly two thousand years to ponder and absorb Christ's teachings. These poor guys are being hit with radical new concepts and insights practically every day. If they tend to look a bit naïve or foolish at times, we should readily admit we probably wouldn't have done any better!

Think about what a roller coaster ride being disciples was for all of them. They've seen and heard remarkable things from the Lord. They've also seen the multitudes flock to Jesus and then turn away. And most recently, they've heard Jesus plainly predict His own demise in Jerusalem. (He talked about his resurrection too, but they seemed to miss that part!) It's not hard to imagine them thinking "This is not turning out at all like we expected! Where are the powerful positions we assumed would be ours in this new Kingdom? And we're certainly not amassing any wealth!"

Some have suggested Simon Peter was being entirely selfish in this instance, questioning from a "what's in it for me?" attitude. That is most likely not the case, especially in view of Simon Peter's statement, which preceded his question. "We have left everything to follow you!" If you think about it, in a way they had done what Jesus suggested to the rich young ruler. They've left their families and put their careers on hold. So while Simon Peter's question had eternal implications, he may have been thinking of physical needs as well.

Jesus assured Simon Peter and the others they would receive a special measure of glory, sitting on twelve thrones, judging the twelve tribes of Israel. And the Lord further states that everyone who has made sacrifices in this life for him will receive a hundred times as much and eternal life to boot!

I don't remember ever considering giving up as a Christian. But many times I've wondered, "What's going to become of me?" Do you remember "Que Sera Sera" (Whatever will be, will be!), the children's song made even more famous by Doris Day? It has a charming little tune and I always liked it, even though I don't agree with its philosophy. Absolute fatalists, as well as some religious people, think of their life as being on something like a giant video-tape, just playing itself out exactly according to a pre-determined script: "Whatever will be, will be!"

I have my own philosophy on this. It basically goes "What and where He wants me to be, I'll try to be!" Sure, I've wondered in my own way "Will I be famous? Will I be rich?" And I'm happy to say that with a long season of growing up (I haven't been a "quick study" in maturing in Christ!), I'm getting more comfortable and happy with the Bible's answers to both questions.

Young preachers (just like many others in any chosen field of endeavor) sometimes dream of achieving widespread recognition and acclaim. I remember sitting in a dormitory room late one night with other "preacher boys" (Bible majors), dreaming of how famous we might be someday. Somehow we came up with a friendly bet about which one of us would be the first one to be invited back to that very college to speak at the annual Bible lectureship. Then wouldn't you know it – a few years later I was invited to speak at the lectureship! Shortly after receiving the invitation, I recalled the discussion in the dorm room, and felt a bit ashamed at the vanity and worldliness it reflected. This was one time I didn't have to struggle with having a big head about being asked to speak. I was sufficiently humbled, just remembering my unworthiness in light of my youthful ambitions. God may or may not have worked directly to get me on that lectureship program, but He surely worked through the occasion to teach me a thing or two about seeking fame. I'm convinced God has allowed me to be just about as famous as I can stand to be.

You may be well on your way in your life's work, and perhaps you are finding sufficient fame and riches, spiritual more so than temporal. If you are in Christ, you are in line to be an heir of incalculable riches. And if you have a few people who genuinely love you, then you can be happy to be famous to them and not worry about whether you are or aren't to anyone else!

If you are a younger person, just launching into your career, please consider this. Don't pursue fame – pursue service. If fame comes, let it be serendipitously and not an achieved goal. It is right to make a living and provide for your family. But approach the acquisition of wealth remembering Paul's words in 1st Timothy 6:9: "People who want to get rich fall into temptation and a trap and into many foolish and harmful desires that plunge men into ruin and destruction." Seek to be rich in love and good works first. Then if God blesses you with wealth, you'll have a better chance of handling it than if you had done it in reverse order.

"These have come so that your faith – of greater worth than gold, which perishes even though refined by fire – may be proved genuine and may result in praise, glory and honor when Jesus Christ is revealed." (1st Peter 1:7)

PRINCIPLE SIX

"Before The Big Test, Pay Attention To The Details"

a. The Attentive Disciple

READ **Mark 11:20-21**

This is a strange tale! Why would the "author of life," the "creator of all things" curse a living thing, causing it to die? In our age of environmental sensitivity, this seems unconscionable. But curse it He did! The next day as Jesus and His disciples retrace their steps out of the city, we're not surprised to see Simon Peter be the one who speaks up, pointing out to the Lord the tree's withered condition.

Before we go on to the more profound lessons in this story, let us take note of Simon Peter's feeling compelled to point out to Jesus the demise of the fig tree. You have to wonder; did Simon Peter think the Lord didn't know the outcome of His statement to the tree? Or, is it just something in him like the enthusiasm of a child wanting to point out everything to his parent, or teacher, or friends? (You may take exception to someone who has a knack for stating the obvious, but they are oftentimes the ones who end up being elected to high offices or running big corporations.)

There was a specific reason Jesus caused this fig tree to die. Did you notice in the text the detail of the tree being "in leaf," although it was not the season for it to have leaves? It was commonly known that when these trees had leaves, they were also to have fruit. Jesus went to pick some of the fruit. (This was not stealing; it was a practice of their culture to have certain crops along the roadsides as a courtesy for travelers.) In effect, this tree was saying one thing and doing another – the standard mode of hypocrisy. Not for a second are we suggesting the tree had a conscious mind, and was deliberately trying to deceive. It was just malfunctioning as a fruit-bearing tree. It was giving off the message there was fruit when there was no fruit, and in the wrong season, to boot!

Some might interpret this as a heartless act on the part of Jesus, something like cruelty to an animal, but that wasn't the case. If Jesus hadn't caused the tree to wither, no doubt the owner would have soon chopped it down. Jesus is pointing out to his disciples the need for consistency and propriety, not hypocrisy. Elsewhere He speaks of unfruitful trees being cut down and thrown into the fire.

For our purposes, the crucial point of the story is Simon Peter's attentiveness to the details. He, along with the others had heard Jesus curse the tree. We don't know if they all noticed the results, but Simon Peter did for sure. There's an important lesson hidden herein if we will notice it. Attentiveness is essential for imitation.

Impressionists, who amuse us with their portrayals of well-known persons, do so by having picked up on some little mannerism or trait most of us would have overlooked.

Imitation is a key ingredient of discipleship. While disciples are learners, they are more than just students. They not only learn from their teachers, they imitate their teachers – their lifestyles, their likes and dislikes, even sometimes their manner of dress or patterns of speech.

It is easy to imagine Simon Peter studying Jesus "like a book." The apostle may not have been well educated, but he knew how to learn. Oh, like with all of us, he struggled to accept all Jesus taught and practiced, but none of the details eluded him. Experts say we learn how to walk, talk and numerous other basic life functions by imitation. The Bible says we learn to "walk in the light" by imitating Jesus (1 John 1:7, 2:6).

I've always been a fairly imitative person. Perhaps like you, I do better when someone shows me how to do something, instead of just telling me. So it is not surprising I draw my greatest spiritual strength from attempting to imitate the characteristics of Jesus. And as much as I can, I also try to emulate the good qualities of some who were close to him, like the apostles. Some people understand the theology first, then the practical. Show me the practical, and then I have a better chance of grasping the academic.

Since none of us were privileged to be eyewitnesses of Jesus, we have to find other ways to "see" him, and thereby be able to imitate him. First, let me emphasize that I do not believe in or advocate at all any kind of "mystical" seeing of the Lord. I have at my disposal the same resources you do – the books of Matthew, Mark, Luke and John. But I do have a technique I employ, and you may find it useful to you, as well.

When I read the accounts of the teachings or conversations or miracles of Jesus, I try to imagine myself as the director of a movie being made about these events. As director, I have to place everyone in certain spots, think about the background scenery, think about the volume and tone in which statements were made, etc. In other words, I try as vividly as possible to play out the whole thing in my head. In so doing, it seems somehow to come alive for me. I try not to miss even the tiniest of details. I suggest you may have to do this for yourself, to some degree or another. How else are you going to imitate Jesus unless you can "see" him, at least in your mind?

In the popular movie "Sister Act 2" Whoopi Goldberg portrays an entertainer pretending to be a nun in a parochial school, where she is the music teacher and choir director. Her oft-repeated phrase to her listless class is "You better wake up and pay attention!" She finally gets through to the kids, and they and the struggling school are helped.

What about you? Are you paying attention to the Lord? Is he trying to get through to you on some important levels, but you are too busy paying attention to other things? No doubt we'd all be better served to be more like Simon Peter in this one area. Pay attention to everything Jesus says. And when something he promises comes true, be childlike in your exuberant joy!

"To this you were called, because Christ suffered for you, leaving you an example, that you should follow in his steps." (1st Peter 2:21)

b. Okay – I'll Take It All!

This is one of the most touching moments between Jesus and the twelve, revealed to us in Scripture. Hours before His own anguish, Jesus shows them the "full extent of his love" in the most humble of fashions. He goes about the lowly business of washing their feet, normally the job of a slave or servant in that culture. As if this is not humbling enough in its own right, as a part of the exercise He washes the feet of Judas, the one He knows will betray him. He washes the feet of the others, knowing they will forsake Him at the moment of His arrest (Mark 14:50). And finally, He knows Simon Peter will deny even knowing Him. Nonetheless, He carries out this great act of servanthood. And in the process He shows them how they are to treat one another. A beautiful story, indeed!

But, as we might expect, our impulsive and outspoken friend Simon Peter can't just let this event happen without a response. Commendable is his concern that Jesus, his Master, not debase himself in such a way. It reminds us of the attitude of John the Baptist when Jesus came to be baptized. John forthrightly stated, "It is you who should baptize me!" No doubt Simon Peter is thinking, "I should be washing your feet." But the apostle should have learned by now that Jesus always had a specific purpose in His actions, and the purpose was always right. With a spirit of obedience, Simon Peter should have accepted the loving gesture, gaining a new insight into the principles of true servanthood.

Simon Peter failed to trust Jesus not just once in this matter, but twice. First he blurts out, "You shall never wash my feet!" Jesus patiently explains if He is not allowed to wash Simon Peter, "you have no part with me." This statement has implications for all believers. It should settle for all time any misconception of anyone's self-righteousness being sufficient to get them into Heaven. A believer, whether these chosen apostles, or us today, has to allow our sin problem to be taken care of by the Lord. We can't provide the remedy for the ravages of our own sins.

Simon Peter's second failure to trust Jesus reaches beyond what Jesus is trying to do and says, "Well, not just my feet, but my whole body." Some people straggle behind, trying to catch up with where God wants them to be. Impetuous people often leap ahead and either want to do too much for God, or have God do more for them than is necessary.

Has it ever occurred to you how your feet may be the most unattended part of your body? This is probably not intentional, but they are the farthest from your reach, your vision, and your nose! And yet your feet are in contact with something, if only the ground, more than any other part of the body. Foot problems can quickly immobilize you! Feet are susceptible to strain, fracture, infection, and filth. Invent a shoe able to relieve stress, as well as aches and pains up through the body, and you'll be fabulously rich!

It is not surprising that Jesus chose the washing of feet to make a much deeper point than just His serving His disciples. The disciples had been made clean (spiritually) through their relationship with Jesus. But even so, they would need throughout their lives additional and frequent small cleansings from any subsequent sins. We shall later discuss the matter of one's initial conversion to Jesus and the process of ongoing conversion which must follow.

Our sins are "washed away" at the time of our initial obeying of the gospel (see Acts 22:16). Inevitably we are going to sin after our conversion, though hopefully less than before. But we do not need to be born again each time we commit a sin. God has provided what's been dubbed "the second law of pardon," as illustrated in the story of Simon the Sorcerer in Acts 8. Recognition of sin, repentance, and prayer are essential ingredients in this restoration of the soul to a right relationship with God.

I had a great-aunt who was fastidious about her fitness and health. At age 80 she could bend over and put both palms flat on the floor (without cheating!). We laughed at her, but she had a custom, which, looking back on it now, may not have been as crazy as we thought. She told us she would take her bath before bedtime, and then carry a wet washcloth with her to her bedroom. The last thing she would do before retiring was to clean her feet. I wish I were as fastidious about remembering every night to ask God to forgive me for my misdeeds during that day.

Where we attend church we eat the Lord's Supper every week, as they did in the early church (Acts 20:7). In addition to remembering Jesus' sacrifice, which is the primary purpose of this memorial meal, I use this as a weekly occasion to make sure I am right with God. While the emblems are being passed is a good time to think about the spiritual occurrences (successes and failures) of the week just passed, and the challenges of the week just beginning.

If you have not learned to allow God to deal with the continuing sin in your life, do so quickly. Allowing sin to go un-confessed and therefore unforgiven makes you increasingly vulnerable to the wiles of the Evil One. This could lead eventually to spiritual disaster. When you are mindful that you have sinned in some specific way, try reading Psalm 51 in a prayerful manner. Let this incredible passage lead you in your own confession of sin and repentance before the Father. Second, learn and remember the principles of 1st John 1:7-9. This should be familiar ground for all who want to maintain a good relationship with God.

And try not to run ahead of God. His plan for your life is exactly what you need. Seek to find His Will, not impose your will upon Him.

"And this water symbolizes baptism that now saves you also – not the removal of dirt from the body but the pledge of a good conscience toward God. It saves you by the resurrection of Jesus Christ," (1st Peter 3:21)

c. Be Careful What You Say; You May Have To Eat Your Words!

READ **Matthew 26:35; Mark 14:29-31; Luke 22:31-34**

In the final evening of Jesus' natural life (prior to his death, burial, and resurrection), He predicted that all of His apostles would fall away that very night. While all protested the very notion, Simon Peter is the most vociferous in affirming his loyalty. He discounts the threats of imprisonment or death – he will not deny Jesus, no matter what! In Mark he even declares his commitment as being beyond any of the others. "Even if all the rest deny you, I won't!"

This is the height of presumption. While claiming his own imperviousness to denying Jesus, he exalts himself at the expense of the others. In other words, he seems to be saying, "These others may not be much, but you can count on me, Lord!"

Luke's account seems to imply Jesus' having some kind of an ongoing dialogue with Satan. "Simon, Simon, Satan has asked to sift you as wheat. But I have prayed for you, that your faith will not fail. And when you have turned back, strengthen your brothers." The points in those two sentences are incredible! First, did you notice Jesus didn't call him Peter (rock), but only by Simon (wavering one)? Second, there's the matter of "sifting like wheat," which we'll discuss momentarily. Third, did you see how Jesus prayed for Simon Peter, even though He knew the outcome? (Do we sometimes stop praying for people too soon, when it appears they have no chance?) Fourth, did you catch Jesus' prophecy about Simon Peter turning back? While the Lord realized Simon Peter's potential for failure, He also saw his potential for ultimate success. And fifth, we wonder if Simon Peter could in any way comprehend Jesus' admonition that Simon Peter should at some point in the future strengthen the others?

Jesus plainly tells Simon Peter that the apostle will deny Him three times before the rooster crows, meaning before sunup.

Have you ever thought or said, "I'll never do that!" only to find yourself later doing the very thing you adamantly avowed was impossible? Or worse yet, after recognizing some sin in your life you've made the bold claim, "I'll never do that again!" Wouldn't you agree that eating our own words is most unpleasant? It is folly for us to think, "Others (particularly so and so over there) may struggle with that kind of sin – but not I!" It is quite humbling when you realize that you have done the very thing you condemned in others.

Let's think about Satan for a moment, not because we want to, but because we must. If Jesus' mission was to "seek and save the lost" (Luke 19:10), what was and is Satan's mission? Jesus said the "the thief" (obviously referring to Satan) "comes only to kill, and steal and destroy" (John 10:10). Jesus told Simon Peter that Satan had asked (permission?) to "sift him like wheat." If we believe we are susceptible to the same temptations as these disciples, this should cause us to shudder. Satan, if we allow him to, can deal with us as dispassionately as a worker does with common grain. Unlike The Father and The Son and The Spirit, who see us as precious ones, the Devil views us only as things to be destroyed.

There was a time in my impetuous and presumptuous youth that I wasn't really afraid of the Devil, although I should have been. I once made the arrogant statement to a group of teenagers, "I wish I could just take the Devil on in a fist fight!" How foolish I was! Now, having learned a little more about the Evil One – having been "sifted" numerous times – I don't want to have anything to do with him. I realize I, by myself, am no match for him at all.

And I've also learned the folly of making great boasts about what I'm going, or not going, to do. James is right when he says, "all such boasting is evil" (James 4:17). All I can do is seek to follow the Lord as best I can, with as much humility as I can muster. And I'll leave the fighting with Satan to the divine Ones who are infinitely more powerful than I. I trust that as I'm "clothed in Christ" and resist the Devil, he will flee (1 Peter 5:8,9)!

Wise men from the past and present advise us to learn to "measure our words." Carefully and thoughtfully make promises to God, and do your best to keep them. The same applies to promises made to people. Work hard at not making "idle boasts" about what you will or won't ever do. By all means, when you realize you have done something you had said you'd never do, confess it quickly to God. And if people have been negatively affected, apologize quickly and sincerely, commit to do better, and go on!

"Be self-controlled and alert. Your enemy the devil prowls around like a roaring lion looking for someone to devour." (1st Peter 5:8)

63

d. Simon, Are You Asleep?

READ **Matthew 26:36-46; Mark 14:32-42**

It was one of Jesus' customs to use the Garden of Gethsemane, on the Mount of Olives near Jerusalem, as a kind of retreat for Himself and His disciples. This is where Judas, the betrayer, expected to find Him. Jesus took Simon Peter, James, and John with Him, and asked them to "keep watch with him." This probably meant to pay attention, possibly even praying as He was praying.

How far can you throw a stone? That's how far Jesus went from them before He fell face downward and began an agonizing period of prayer. The "sweat drops as of blood" are a well-known testimony of the intensity of His petitions. The prayers recorded for us are profound in their reverence and passion. But these three who accompanied Him, because they were so sleepy, missed most of these incredible moments.

We could reason that it was very late in the night – no doubt past their normal bedtime. Jesus' words during the Last Supper had saddened them (Mark 14:19). Luke (a physician) records they were "exhausted from sorrow" (Luke 22:45). As many of you know, there is no fatigue like what is often felt after a period of grief.

Upon the second of these awakenings, Jesus speaks directly to Simon Peter asking, "Simon, are you asleep? Could you not keep watch for one hour?" He implores them a third time to "watch and pray." The Lord's concern here is "that you will not fall into temptation." He knows what vexing things lie immediately ahead. And He gives them the words so often quoted in our world, "The spirit is willing, but the body is weak." The encouragement didn't work. As He returns from his ordeal a third time, He finds them again having succumbed to sleep.

Okay, we can make excuses for them, but come on! This is the defining hour of Jesus' ministry. He has been telling them for months to expect these events. There are just some times in life when one has to gear up and press themselves beyond the routine, beyond the normal limits. Failure to discern those crucial moments will result in an ineffective and unproductive life. These three disciples were given an opportunity to observe incredibly private and intense moments between the Son of God and The Father, and they were sleeping!

Some people pretty much sleepwalk through life, being given the opportunity to see and understand, but missing the most extraordinary things. You don't want to be one of those people, do you?

I'm a little surprised at Simon Peter in this story. I would have thought his impetuous, inquisitive nature would have driven him not to miss a thing. But it didn't. I trust he later realized what he'd missed and worked hard not to be "asleep at the wheel" of his life ever again.

I learned a valuable lesson while our Anita and Matt were still small and at home. While attending a seminar for ministers, one of the speakers urged those of us with families to make a commitment to "spiritual 'Miller Time,'" based upon the heavy advertising campaign being run at the time by the Miller Brewing Company. (Why has the best advertising in TV history always been the beer commercials?) His point was for us to think about the first fifteen minutes when we come home from work. Instead of coming in, plopping down and more or less claiming "my time" to relax (hopefully without the beer!), he suggested a more productive use of those special moments. He implored us to "gear up" past the demands of the day and the grind of the traffic getting home, and to really give ourselves fully to our spouses and kids for about fifteen minutes, then relax. It was some of the best advice I ever got! Sure I was usually tired when I got home, and often my nerves were frayed. But Francie and the kids got used to the special attention I gave them when I first got home, and I think it enriched our family forever. You don't want to "wake up" and realize what you've missed with your kids after they've gone.

All of our lives are full of opportunities to be more attentive, more sensitive, more involved. Most who reach old age have some regrets for certain things they did, but more often they have regrets for things they could have done, but didn't. Sit down soon and write out a life plan for the good and positive things you hope will have happened with your spouse, your children, your friends and God – and then get busy making that list a reality! Most of your greatest accomplishments in life will have been done when you had to gear up to get beyond your normal limits and really live!

"The end of all things is near. Therefore be clear minded and self-controlled so that you can pray." (1st Peter 4:7)

PRINCIPLE SEVEN

"Learning From Failures is the Best Way to Become a Success"

a. A Different Kind of Barber

READ Matthew 26:51; Mark 14:47; Luke 22:50; John 18:10

This had to be a wild scene! Were you ever in a situation where everything was happening so quickly, you couldn't even figure out what all had happened until much later? Surely this was just such a moment.

Earlier in the evening Jesus had somewhat perplexed the apostles with His remarks leading up to and within what we now call the "last supper." From there He had taken Simon Peter, James and John with Him to the garden. While the Lord struggled in prayer, they struggled, unsuccessfully, to stay awake. And now suddenly all madness seemingly breaks loose. A group, armed with clubs and swords, arrives to arrest Jesus. Judas betrays the Master with a kiss. As they seize Jesus, a bizarre incident takes place. Malchus, one in the arresting party and a servant of the High Priest, has his ear cut off by one of Jesus' companions. If you didn't know which disciple, you could probably guess!

Barbers work dangerously close to some awfully sensitive and vital parts of our necks and heads, and usually with some potentially lethal instruments. One of the most dreaded events, from the perspective of both the giver and receiver, is to have one's ear cut while receiving a haircut. Well, our friend Simon Peter didn't just nick someone's ear – he lopped it right off. And, as we shall see, removing the ear must have been for Simon Peter, at least for a moment, something of a disappointment.

Luke's record reveals earlier in the evening an interesting dialogue between Jesus and the disciples regarding their future mission trips (see Luke 22:36-38). As strange as it may seem, He even advised them to obtain a sword if they didn't have one. At that point the disciples said, "See, Lord, here are two swords." And Jesus replied with "That is enough." (This passage is a mystery to most commentators, and to me!) They immediately left for the garden, and we tend to forget about the swords, until later.

Not all of the four Gospels always report the same specific events. And when they do, there is always variation in the details. For example, only Luke (a physician) records Jesus healing the man's ear. The first three Gospels only mention "one of Jesus' companions" as taking this violent step. But John identifies the swordsman as Simon Peter.

You can be fully assured Simon Peter wasn't aiming for poor Malchus' ear. He wasn't thinking, "Now I'll teach this guy a lesson with a little cosmetic surgery." He, no doubt, aimed to split the man's head right in two. Either Malchus ducked or Simon Peter had a bad aim, but the ear was off.

In this incident, Simon Peter is undeniably courageous, but perhaps at the same time a bit faithless. He had said earlier "Even if I have to die with you, I will never disown you." In full view of being outnumbered and under-equipped, he was willing to die on the spot defending his Lord. But we must remember several times Jesus has told all of them He must be arrested and eventually killed. Simon Peter's raw humanity, impetuousness and all, wells up in a desperate act, which he probably later realized was foolish. The recurring theme of 1st Peter, written some 30 years later, is how to bear up under unjust suffering.

Have you ever let your temper, even in the name of "righteous indignation," actually keep you from doing and being what God would want in a certain situation? We all have. As we mature, in situations where we would have (metaphorically) "reached for a sword" through our words or actions, hopefully we learn to bear up patiently.

I have, in jocular fashion, several times compared myself to Simon Peter. But this incident reminds me of one of my weaknesses. While reacting to something that is wrong, I have responded in ways equally wrong, or worse. I'm not a "striker" (to use a King James Version word), at least not with my hand or a weapon. But angry words are almost always hurtful weapons. Unfortunately we cannot undo our mistakes, although by the grace of God they can be forgiven. Fortunately, we can mature if we learn from our experiences. This seems to take us impetuous ones a little longer. (Hey, getting older is not such a bad thing!)

It's sometimes hard to take Jesus at His word – to turn the other cheek, to return blessing for insult, or to rejoice and be glad in the face of persecution. It is also sometimes very difficult to remember the big picture of God's Will, realizing that living for Him will not always be rosy or fancy-free.

Pray. Pray a lot! Pray about the way you react to injustices to others or yourself. And imitate Jesus!

"When they hurled their insults at him, he did not retaliate; when he suffered, he made no threats. Instead, he entrusted himself to him who judges justly." (1st Peter 2:23)

b. Ol' "Wavering Rock" Personified

READ **Matthew 26:58-74; Mark 14:54-72;
Luke 22:54-60; John 18:15-27**

Among the many titles the Lord Jesus could wear, one would certainly be prophet. On numerous occasions in the Gospels He demonstrated his ability to foretell the immediate future. Nowhere is Jesus' prophetic gift more dramatically demonstrated than in the three denials by Simon Peter.

One of the things that made Simon Peter so special is the combination of courage (which some might call foolhardiness!) and faith. We've seen him walk toward Jesus on the water, make bold assertions of faith, draw the sword in the face of insurmountable odds, etc. All of the apostles momentarily scattered when Jesus was arrested. Most went and hid. Simon Peter and John follow "at a distance." (That probably means a safe distance, which is understandable.) Although this is not the greatest demonstration of faith, it is certainly well beyond the faith of their peers.

In all four of the Gospels the emphasis is on Simon Peter's words and actions during these intense moments. As you read the accounts of how he is recognized and/or suspected as being one of Jesus' associates, you see the apostle showing increasing uncertainty. Right when he would have least expected it his faith is waning. With each conversation, and each subsequent answer, his denials become more adamant.

It is in this episode we see Simon Peter totally living up to his name. Following Jesus after he was arrested, he was being a "rock." Denying Jesus at the crucial moment, he was merely the "wavering one."

Simon Peter was probably in a state of total confusion. He didn't want to be denying Jesus, but he was. He was being somewhat courageous, but feeling terribly afraid. He knew what he believed, but did he? One way to look at this, giving Simon Peter the benefit of the doubt is this: this was new ground; he had never been put into such a position before. Sometimes when we face first-time adversity in an area of our lives, we do well. At other times, we don't fare so well!

For a moment, let's look ahead into what we know about this apostle in the coming weeks, months and years of his life. Never again, even in life-threatening situations, do we see him denying his association with or faith in Jesus. He learned well from this experience. Oh that we could likewise learn from our spiritual failures, no matter how disturbing or embarrassing they were at the moment.

I can't recall a time when I have denied, when asked the direct question, being a follower of Jesus Christ. But I can just as honestly say I know there have been many times when I could have spoken up for Christ, but remained mute. So my denials, though not as dramatic as Simon Peter's, were just as real. I am trying to grow out of this. If you can relate similar "indirect denials," would you join me in trying to do better?

Since proclaiming is the opposite of denying, learn how to proclaim (announce) your relationship with Christ in little, everyday situations. This is not to suggest you have to become a street preacher, or even make yourself an annoyance by always bringing up your religion in a way most people consider pushy. Just wait and listen for those little opportunities that come along in conversations where you can quietly announce your faith. They do come up! In response to, "What did you do this weekend?" You answer, "We did some housework, rented a movie, went to church, and grilled hot dogs." Or after, "How did you feel after hearing about that disaster?" you say, "I felt sad and prayed for the people involved."

Each time you let it be known you are a Christian, even in some seemingly benign statement, you are overcoming your fear of being ashamed of belonging to Christ. (See Romans 1:16.) As this kind of "confessing" of Christ becomes more and more your lifestyle, you also become less and less likely of ever denying Him.

"That you may declare the praises of him who called you out of darkness into his wonderful light." (1st Peter 2:9)

c. The Look

READ **Luke 22:61**

We respond to looks from others. Most of us eventually get around to admitting we were blessed in having a mother who could give us "the look." In America, most kids know things are getting serious when their mom uses their full name – "Keith Scott Hodges, you come here this instant!" But that's nothing compared to "the look!" That look can cause one's blood to run cold, the hair on the back of their neck to bristle, and breathing to become very shallow.

Likewise, some schoolteachers have a reputation that precedes them for giving "the look." Or our hearts fluttered the first time some cute thing or hunk gave us a look that let us know they were interested. All great actors, and especially comedians, can say more with a look than with a page of script. And part of having one as a friend, especially your spouse, is being able to read the look on their face.

At his moment of highest ever anxiety, Simon Peter got a special "look" from Jesus. Just when the cursing, adamant apostle was swearing he knew nothing of Jesus, from the other side of the courtyard the Lord "turned and looked at him." That "look" said more to Peter than a hundred of Jesus' sermons. His heart was appropriately broken. Try to imagine the anguish he felt as he came face to face with the reality of his denial. He had sworn he would never deny Jesus, even if all the rest did. And now, he had done just exactly what Jesus had prophesied: denied Him three times before the rooster finished its crowing.

There are three ways in which any of us can be personally convicted of a sinful action or attitude. It can be impressed upon us personally by another Christian, or in hearing a sermon, or in a private reading of the Word. When I am aware of this happening to me, it not only stirs my soul, but it sometimes even affects me physically. I sense what seems to be a burning sensation throughout my upper body and face. I don't believe this is anything miraculous; just my body reacting to the pain my mind and spirit is feeling. It has taken me a long time, but I have learned it is not profitable in any way to ignore this reaction. I can't really be happy when there is unrepented sin in my life. While it is good to realize I'm sinning less and less, I know I'll never totally outgrow my sinful nature. That's why 1 John 1:7-10 is so precious to me. And I hope I never lose the capacity to see (with the eye of faith) the "look" of Jesus through fellow Christians or the Word.

None of us will ever experience, in this realm, literal eye contact with Jesus, as Simon Peter did that morning in the courtyard. But each of us who are serious about our spiritual lives eventually comes face to face with the reality of our sins. We'll hear the words of Jesus, or one of His apostles or prophets, and we'll be convicted, cut to the heart. There will be a day – judgment day – when we'll see the Lord, and He will see us. He'll look to see whether or not "he really ever knew us" (Matthew 7:23), and whether or not we came to the judgment "clothed in Him" (2 Corinthians 5:2-4; Galatians 3:27). Will you be ready for His piercing gaze?

"And the God of all grace, who called you to his eternal glory in Christ, after you have suffered a little while, will himself restore you and make you strong, firm and steadfast." (1st Peter 5:10)

d. Bitter Tears

READ **Matthew 26:75; Mark 14:72; Luke 22:62**

When Jesus turned and looked at Simon Peter it must have, as the old saying goes, hit him like a ton of bricks. He was overwhelmed with the full realization of his denials. The text says he went out and wept bitterly.

Let's take a few moments to try to explode two myths.

The first is that real men don't cry. This discussion goes round and round endlessly! Right now our society seems to be in something of a sensitivity mode. So we're hearing lots about how wonderful it is if men can cry. That hasn't always been the sentiment, and it will probably continue to go back and forth for all time. "Jesus wept" (John 11:35). Who would suggest that either the Lord or Simon Peter were anything less than real men? Crying at this crucial moment was absolutely necessary in order for Simon Peter to be able to go on.

Compare the reaction of Simon Peter to that of Judas Iscariot, the betrayer of Jesus. The Bible says Judas was remorseful (some versions even read "repented"), and said, "I have sinned" in reference to his betrayal. But the Bible says nothing about any tears. He went out and hanged himself. In contrast, Simon Peter wept bitterly, but eventually rose from his anguish to serve again.

But notice also that crying does not prove how spiritual one is. Neither does being unemotional or cracking jokes at crucial times necessarily mean that one is strong. As the wise teacher wrote so long ago, "There is a time to weep, and a time to laugh" (Ecclesiastes 3:4). One of those right times to weep is when you are made fully, even painfully, aware of your sin. This is true whether you're female or male.

Have you ever wept over your sins? If not, why not? Do you think your sins aren't really that bad? Or could it be that you have not taken an honest look at the true ugliness of your sins and sinfulness?

A second myth that needs to be exploded is the idea of total conversion occurring at one decisive moment in time. Oh, there's "the hour I first believed," as the song "Amazing Grace" so eloquently conveys. Even if you've been preparing for it for years, there's a specific moment in time when you obey the Lord in faith and become his child. But genuine conversion to the Lord also has to happen over a lifetime. For any growing disciple there will surely be numerous mini-conversions occurring at numerous points in one's life and faith. It's like we move to a whole new depth of insight or understanding, prompted by some life crisis, or become more fully aware of some Biblical truth.

This was what happened to Simon Peter. One way to look at all these episodes is to see them as a series of these mini-conversions. Sure, he had made the big decision to follow Jesus. But by necessity, as he learned and grew, he needed to make many more changes (conversions) to become more like Christ.

This does not mean every time we have one of these ongoing conversions we have to (a) discredit everything we've learned or decided before, or (b) be re-baptized. A young woman was recently overheard saying she had just been "reborn again, for the second time." (Was she thinking she had been born again three times?) No such language or action occurs in Scripture. We do well when we try to avoid making the gospel more complex!

Repentance should be seen more as a lifestyle than as a once-and-done experience. Perhaps like you, there have been crucial moments in my Christian life when I've been prompted to tears over my sins and sinfulness. It was necessary, and I'm glad I could do it. It will, no doubt, have to happen again. It's not something I try to create, nor do I feel I have to do it on some regular basis. But when the need is real, I want it to be able to happen.

A part of fully understanding the gospel is looking realistically at your past and present sins. Your sense of being forgiven will be rather shallow if you deny yourself this realization. And when as a Christian you've really blown it, don't kill yourself spiritually. Rather let the tears of remorse come. "Godly sorrow leads to repentance" (2 Corinthians 7:10). And after the tears, then, like Simon Peter, be ready for more service in the Kingdom.

True spiritual growth is so exciting ... and so necessary! Never limit the potential for some new level of conversion to be stifled by thinking you've arrived. Faith needs to be seen not so much as a destination, but as an ongoing journey. You will only reach the state of fully converted when the Lord perfects you in Heaven.

"He is patient with you, not wanting anyone to perish, but everyone to come to repentance." (2nd Peter 3:9)

PRINCIPLE EIGHT

"God Doesn't Want You to Quit Just Because You Failed"

a. Go Tell Peter

READ **Mark 16:7**

Don't you know the three days (or parts of three days) between the crucifixion and the time Simon Peter heard of Jesus' resurrection were torturous for the apostle? Like the rest of Jesus' followers, he was confused, disappointed, and scared. But for Simon Peter, there was the additional gnawing pain of his denial. He had been so confident in his assertions of how he would never deny Jesus and was willing to die with Him. But at the crucial moment he had melted like wax in bright sunlight!

The time Jesus' body was in the tomb must have been like an entombment for Simon Peter as well. The Savior may have been well aware of this, and we can assume it was the Lord himself who instructed the angel to tell the women to "go tell Peter" along with the other disciples.

While all the disciples initially disbelieved the report, Simon Peter must have been surprised and relieved at the same time. Not only is there the thrilling news of the Lord's resurrection, but also he has been specifically named as one of the first ones to be told. This is the first stage of Simon Peter's reinstatement.

We can only imagine what the apostle must have been thinking. If he had any confidence Jesus actually would be raised from the dead, he was probably thinking the Lord was certainly finished with him! How many times can one blow it and not be dismissed as unworthy? This is probably the very reason the angel, in commanding all the disciples be told, specified Simon Peter. It's going to take a lot to convince Simon Peter that the Lord wants anything more to do with him.

Simon Peter knew, factually, of Jesus' capacity to forgive over and over. He was the very one who asked Jesus about how many times one should forgive and heard the Lord's stunning answer of "seventy times seven." But emotionally it was hard to believe. Does this remind you of yourself? Sometimes after we've transgressed, even though we know of the Lord's forgiving nature, we can't believe He would actually forgive us one more time.

One more point needs to be made here. We have a tendency to think of forgiveness just from our perspective – need! We must also try to consider it from the Lord's perspective – desire. God wants to forgive us. When He sees us grieving over our sins, His heart is stirred. Jesus wanted to have Simon Peter reinstated. He knew of the apostle's bitter tears and weekend of grief. One of the most amazing statements in all the Bible is surely "This is good, and pleases God our Savior, who wants all men to be saved and to come to a knowledge of the truth" (1Timothy 2:3,4). Even after all our sins against Him, His Word, and other people, God still wants us to be saved!

We had a dog that was something of an escape artist. In spite of our constant efforts to keep him in our yard, he would escape and terrorize the neighborhood (plus violate the local leash laws). He would never harm a child, but he did other things not appreciated by those around us. One day he was gone and did not return. We figured he had left for good. A couple of days later we got a message from the local animal shelter. He had been caught and was waiting there to be claimed by us, adopted by someone else, or be put to sleep. I loved the dog, but had reluctantly decided, "This is it! We just can't keep having this bother." I went to the shelter with our daughter Anita, who was about thirteen at the time, to say goodbye. (You know what's coming!) We saw Sport and she left the shelter sobbing. I, already being upset, began to cry with her. So we marched back into the shelter and claimed our pet. Tears turned to joy as he rode home with us. I promised Anita, and later our son Matt, somehow we would try harder to find a way to keep him contained. "Necessity is the mother of invention." We did find a way, and we kept him, without any more escapes, for the rest of his life.

Now see, our dog wasn't as much a part of his redemption as we were. While he seemed happy to see us, his being restored to us didn't mean as much to him as it did to us. Don't you think each of us is more valuable to God than any of our beloved pets are to us? And don't you think the Father is infinitely happier, even than we are, when we're saved from our sins?

One of the great challenges of living the Christian life is to never lose the sense of awe at God's mercy. ("Unfathomable" is the way Phillips translated it in Romans 11). But at the same time we must never take His mercy for granted or consider it as a license for sinful living.

"Once you were not a people, but now you are the people of God; once you had not received mercy, but now you have received mercy." (1st Peter 2:10)

b. Seeing Is (Not Always) Believing

READ **John 20:3-9**

Mary Magdalene is one of the first ones to see the empty tomb. No doubt in a state of bewilderment, she runs to Simon Peter and John. Upon hearing the news they both set out running to the tomb. The younger John (according to tradition, maybe only a teenager) outran the middle-aged (possibly not in great shape!) Simon Peter. John waits at the entrance of the tomb, perhaps in deference to Simon Peter's age or leadership status, or simply in fear. But he does sneak a peak inside!

Finally Simon Peter comes lumbering up. (The Bible does not say this; it's my mental picture of the scene.) When Simon Peter arrives, he barges right in! There's no saying to John, "You arrived here first; please go on in." He zooms right past John as if he's not even standing there! Let's give Simon Peter the benefit of the doubt. He was probably focused on one thing – seeing exactly what was and wasn't in that tomb. After Simon Peter is inside, John joins him.

Many have concluded this was just another case of Simon Peter's impetuous nature on display. Impetuous people will sometimes forget their manners in areas like going first, speaking up first, etc. It's important for us to remember when God converts someone, He doesn't automatically strip them of their personality and nature. God would have no reason not to allow us to work through the personality and nature He originally gave us. If we've developed an attitude or actions which are sinful or detrimental, those should be discarded, but not the personality. Simon Peter probably always retained, at least to some extent, his take-charge nature. Of course, we'll see later in his life how this was tempered with better judgment and patience.

All they find inside is conclusive evidence Jesus is not there! Oh yes, there's the burial cloth and strips of linen. But for all they knew, the body was stolen, as Mary Magdalene had suggested. The passage plainly says they still did not understand from Scripture (as well as the fact the Lord had plainly told them several times) that Jesus had to rise from the dead.

That evening all of the apostles, except Thomas who was elsewhere, were in a locked room and Jesus appeared to them (John 20:19-29). There were to be numerous times when Jesus would appear to Simon Peter, all of the apostles, more than five hundred followers at one time, to James (Jesus' half-brother who became a

78

leader in the early church), and finally, years later, to the Apostle Paul (1 Corinthians 15:5-8).

But let's go back to that early morning scene with Simon Peter and John at the empty tomb. Even though the text says John "believed," it is hard to know whether this means he believed Jesus had in fact been raised from the dead, or just that he believed the body was not there. (As hard as it seems to be to understand, various passages reveal that some of the apostles, perhaps even all of them, had doubts about his resurrection right up until the time He ascended into Heaven.) At the very least, here they were being prepared to believe. Later Jesus would reveal himself to them in all His post-resurrection glory.

If you think about it long enough, you could probably start listing lots of things God was doing in your life before you became a believer, all to help prepare you for coming to faith.

The earliest conversation I remember having with anyone about anything very significant was with my mother. And it was about death and faith.

I remember it was a summer day and the wind was blowing through the huge trees in our front yard. Since we didn't have air-conditioning, my mother and sister and I were outside taking advantage of the shade and the breeze. A lady from church stopped by to tell us an elderly woman in our congregation had died that day. This was the first time I realized people we love die, and someday I would die. I remember being scared and crying. My mom consoled me as only moms can. She told me two things I have never forgotten. First she said, "Keith, this is why we have our faith, to help us deal with things like this." (That was profound then, and has only grown in its magnitude ever since!) Then to help me feel a little better, she gave me very practical reassurance. She said, "I'm sure you will live at least ten thousand more days." I don't know, but I suspect this was just a number she came up with on the spot. But, to a kid a day is a long time, and ten thousand days seems forever! It occurred to me a few years ago that Mother was promising me I'd probably live until I was about thirty-three! But at the moment, it worked! I felt better and stopped crying. But I never forgot the incident.

I can't prove it, but I believe this incident was provided by God, working through my mother and everyday circumstances, to help lay not only a foundation for my own faith but a basic understanding for ministry. Ministers talk about death a lot in the course of preaching, counseling the dying, and comforting the bereaved. One who hopes to be effective must be equipped to reasonably discuss this difficult issue.

An important resource we all have, but one which many don't tap into very much, are our memories. Try to remember incidents in your life, perhaps long before you made your decision to commit to Christ, which helped shape your thinking toward that end. This can be a thrilling exercise – seeing how God was working with you and on you, perhaps long before you actually heard (or paid attention to) the gospel.

"I think it is right to refresh your memory as long as I live in the tent of this body" (2nd Peter 1:13)

c. He Was Willing To Hang Out the 'Gone Fishin' Sign, But More Training Was Needed

READ **John 21:3**

After His resurrection, Jesus appeared to the apostles and others several times. Scripture specifically says He appeared "to Peter, and then to the Twelve" (1 Corinthians 15:5). These appearances went on for a period of 40 days. Nonetheless, right in the midst of this exciting time, Simon Peter inexplicably states to several of the apostles, "I'm going out to fish." As a strange testimony to his leadership characteristics, they said, "We'll go with you."

Why go fishing now? Surely it wasn't just to relax! From the story that follows we can easily figure out they went back to work – back to their pre-disciple occupation. If you can figure that one out, you can also probably explain why a thinking person would leave the Kingdom of God to return to the world!

Some have commented this was the completion of Jesus' instructions for His disciples to meet Him in Galilee after is resurrection (Matthew 28:10; Mark 16:7). And they were, probably unwittingly, fulfilling that command. However, the surprise they will express at seeing Jesus tends to dismiss any notion this was deliberate obedience.

Jesus wasn't through with Simon Peter yet! One more dynamic conversation had to occur before Simon Peter would emerge as the confident never-to-turn-back-again leader of the apostles and the early church. We shall explore that conversation later.

This episode reminds us again of how many times each of us may have to be reclaimed by Jesus before we are ready to fulfill His purposes in our lives.

I sometimes wonder how many times I have just one more thing to learn before I'm really ready to do what God wants me to do. Of course, I honestly know I already have at my disposal sufficient spiritual knowledge and all the resources I need to be doing His Will right now! But I would like to be in the midst of learning that one more thing on the last day of my life.

If you're trusting in yourself, you will probably turn back just short of doing unimaginably great things for God. But when you trust the Lord, you live with a sense of anticipation that your shining moment for God is just around the next corner. (Oftentimes you won't have recognized those shining moments until long after they've happened!) So please don't decide to hang out the "gone fishin'" sign just before the Master has something great for you to do!

"It would have been better for them not to have known the way of righteousness, than to have known it and then to turn their backs on the sacred command that was passed on to them." (2nd Peter 3:21)

d. Another Big Fish Tale

READ **John 21:3b-14**

Try to imagine this bizarre story. A lone figure stands in the eerie pre-dawn light on the shore of a large inland sea. Nearby is a small charcoal fire with fish and bread slowly cooking. Those who should have most easily recognized Him didn't. (It's amazing what we don't see when we're not expecting to see anything!) The lone figure calls out to weary fishermen, returning from an unsuccessful night of professional fishing. He asks a question in a way that indicates He already knows the answer. Then He offers a suggestion that's seemingly too simple. (How many fishermen do you know who just love for someone to tell them how to fish?) But they dutifully follow the suggestion, and behold there's an amazing catch!

At this moment something is stirred within John – the voice, perhaps – or more likely the realization he'd seen this scenario before! John tells Simon Peter, "It's the Lord!" You will not be surprised, at least not much, by Simon Peter's reaction. He puts on his outer garment, jumps into the water and swims the 100 yards or so to shore. The rest of the disciples bring in the boat, towing the large catch behind, still in the net. Jesus asks for more fish to add to his barbecue, at which time Simon Peter reenters the boat and single-handedly retrieves the net full of fish. The catch was so large the nets should have torn, but didn't.

Tradition has passed down Simon Peter was a large fellow. This story seems to verify the point. He personally manhandles a load several others seemingly struggled to successfully bring in.

This story is rife with irony. There's a large catch of fish, as occurred early in the ministry. Then there's the fish and bread, like in the feedings of the multitudes. A charcoal fire, like the one at which Simon Peter warmed himself, just before one of his denials. There's even a similarity to the Last Supper, when he hands them the bread of this meal. It seems Jesus is drawing tight all the loose ends of so many of the gospel experiences.

If there's any rebuke by Jesus for either going fishing or not readily recognizing Him, it's not recorded. Rather we sense a kindly scene. The master is once again serving and teaching and consoling the disciples.

But there is still one bit of unfinished business with Simon Peter.

I think while we modern disciples await our chance to actually see the face and hear the voice of Jesus, we have to, somehow or other, latch on to something from the message to make Jesus more personal to us. For me, it's this story. Oh, I realize this is not one of the great miracles, or great sermons, or even one of those extremely dramatic events like Jesus' arrest or crucifixion. It's just a minor incident. But as comparably insignificant as it may seem to others, somehow it hits me right where I live.

Just like the disciples must have felt after they "scattered like sheep" at Jesus' arrest, I've felt rather impish in the presence of various ones with whom I have behaved badly. Sometimes those who could have and should have been done with me have just quietly welcomed me back into their good graces. In this story the good shepherd gently gathers up the wandering sheep one last time.

He hosts his own little farewell dinner – not presumptuously, but with humility. He gave the boys a cookout. I love that! I like campfires and barbecues. I like to imagine myself sitting in a circle with the apostles, around that little charcoal fire, eating the piping hot fish and bread, wide-eyed and hanging on every word of the Master. For me right now it's the best way I have to emotionally connect with Jesus. It makes me want to go to Heaven even more!

A wise saying is "One of the ugliest things in the world is ingratitude." When someone gives you grace – kindness you don't deserve – accept it humbly. And then honor their grace to you by showing grace to others. Have a cookout for some knuckleheads you know, treating them like they're the greatest people in the world.

"Though you have not seen him, you love him" (1st Peter 1:8).

PRINCIPLE NINE

"God's Restoration Process Is Necessary"

a. Do You Really Love Me, Simon?

READ John 21:15-17

Yes, there is one more element to the restoration process of Simon Peter. The grace the Lord has shown all the apostles is encouraging and endearing. But even in the midst of grace, sometimes certain issues need to be addressed so they don't resurface.

We might wonder if Simon Peter would have emerged as the fearless and powerful leader we see in the book of Acts had this final dialogue between Jesus and Simon Peter not occurred.

Notice first the series of three questions addressed to Simon Peter. Some have suggested this corresponded to the three denials by the apostle. Notice also the particular use of the word "love" in this passage.

The English language falls far short in comparison with the Greek language, as it relates to the word love. In English, one word has to describe everything from how we feel about our favorite ice cream flavor, to sex, to charity, to family devotion, to our commitment to God! The Greeks had four words for love. I shall attempt to briefly describe these four "loves" in the Greek language.

1. "Eros" – although this is the word from which we get modern words like erotic and erotica, it is not necessarily a dirty word. But it does indicate a very selfish, self-seeking and self-serving kind of love, or desire. This word does not occur in the Bible.
2. "Storge" – love based on familiarity, or commonness of experience. This is most notably family love. Also it could be used to describe the kind of loyalty and affection one might feel for a teammate, fellow-soldier, or coworker.
3. "Phileo" – brotherly love, or friendship. Sometimes translated "affection," this kind of love is for someone you really like.
4. "Agape" – the highest and most noble kind of love. This is the way God loves people. This is not a love of emotion or affection, but a love of deliberate choice (as in loving an enemy!).

Eros is the dynamic of puppy love or lust – not the kind of love on which, for example, to build a marriage. All lasting and healthy relationships will have elements of the other three forms of love. In other words, true love – not just romantic infatuation or casual friendship – must have both elements of emotion and deliberate choice.

As it is recorded in the Greek text, Jesus twice asks Simon Peter if he loves Him (agape). Twice Simon Peter answers he loves him (phileo). Both men knew exactly what they were saying. Jesus was asking if the apostle loved Him with the highest and noblest kind of love. Simon Peter was answering him, in effect, with "I like you a lot!"

The third time Jesus asks, "Do you love me (phileo)?" This cut deep, and Simon Peter knows it! This time Jesus is, in effect, asking, "Do you even like me, Simon?"

In our Biblical text, the issue may seem to have gone unresolved. Only later do we see its lasting affect in this way: Simon Peter never again gave anyone any reason to doubt he loved (agape) Jesus with anything less than his whole heart, soul, mind, and strength.

I had a girlfriend (long before I met my wife!) who constantly asked me, "Do you really love me?" Truth is I liked her a lot, was glad she was my girlfriend, and was open to the possibility it might grow into something more significant later on. I was too young to make a permanent commitment, but I knew what she wanted to hear, so I told her I loved her. This wasn't really a lie; I just gave her a "shallow" answer, but . . . . Ok, I lied: referring to our list above, I loved her with a combination of the first three in the list, not a combination of the last three.

In the earlier years of our marriage my wife frequently asked, "Do you really love me?" To this I could honestly say, "Yes!" Fortunately by the time I married her I was ready to make a deeper commitment, one that involved agape love as well as friendship. It has occurred to me that Francie hasn't asked me that question in a long time. (I think it is still important to tell her frequently, even though she doesn't ask.) I hope that she knows that after 35 years of marriage, I do love her in all the ways that matter most and that my love grows with the passage of time.

Marriage is the greatest commitment we make to another person. Following Christ is even more ultimate. Both relationships, in order to really work, require true love. You won't absolutely be in love with your sweetheart every waking moment of your life. You'll have to choose to love (agape) numerous times to make it work and they'll have to do the same with you. More importantly, you'll have to learn to love God and Christ and The Spirit when it's not fun, not easy, and not pleasant. But the rewards of loving this way, in both arenas, are incredible.

"Above all, love each other deeply, because love covers over a multitude of sins." (1st Peter 4:8)

b. Feed the Sheep

READ John 21:15-17

As a subplot to this story of Simon Peter's reinstatement, we have the interesting personal charge from Jesus regarding the care of the sheep. At the conclusion of each of the questions and answers between Jesus and Simon Peter, there's a word about the sheep, each time slightly different. First, it's "Feed my lambs." Then it's "Take care of my sheep." And finally it's "Feed my sheep."

The idea of God's people being like sheep, "the sheep of his pasture," is well developed in the Old Testament, especially in the Psalms and the Prophets. Jesus identified himself in John chapter 10 as "the good shepherd" and "the true shepherd of the sheep." Jesus referred to sheep several times in his teaching and parables. When Paul was addressing the Ephesian elders, he exhorted them regarding their "shepherding" (Acts 20:28-29). Jesus' teaching was not lost on Simon Peter. In his first letter he exhorted his fellow elders to "be shepherds of God's flock, that is under your care" (1 Peter 5:2).

In case you haven't thought about it, fishermen and shepherds have very dissimilar professions. Although none of us will ever be apostles, and a relative few will ever be "shepherds of God's flock" (elders), all Christians are called, to some degree at least, to be "fishers of men" (evangelistic) and to care about and watch out for our fellow Christians (shepherd-like).

In all of our dealings with people, and especially with fellow Christians, we must be ever seeking to remove those artificial barriers that tend to separate people. "In Christ, there is neither Jew or Greek, slave or free, male or female" (Galations 3:28). In both our outreach to the lost and fellowship with the saved, there should never be reluctance to extend ourselves to ones in different professions, social strata, age groups, etc. People may not always accept you and your convictions about Christ. But it should never be because they sense you are reluctant to be with them because they are different from you. If a crusty old fisherman can develop the heart of a shepherd, then we can too, in time, learn to minister to anybody.

At my first ministerial job after college, one of the members of the congregation was S.A. Bell, an elderly preacher and retired Christian college Bible professor. Brother Bell was very feeble, mostly deaf, and would often appear to fall asleep during the services – only to comment later on the sermon. I also remember he had an unusually firm handshake, which I appreciated. While we were there, Brother Bell grew very weak and was close to death. It was determined he was just as well off at home as he would have been at a hospital. I was asked to take a turn sitting with him through the night. When I arrived at his house, he was sleeping, and I doubted he even knew I was there. Deep in the night, about three in the morning, he suddenly woke up, looked straight at me and said, "Keith, feed the lambs." I was surprised he said spoken to me by name, and especially at what he had said. Before I could respond he said, "Did you hear me Keith? Feed the lambs!" I said, "Yes, Brother Bell, I heard you. You said for me to feed the lambs." He said, "That's right!" He turned over, laughed heartily for several seconds, and then went back to sleep. He never really regained consciousness, and died a few days later.

I've often wondered about what happened that night, how it happened, and why it happened. I'm not inclined to see a miracle in every occurrence. But I do know I can't read about Jesus telling Simon Peter to "feed the sheep" without thinking of this incident. Whether my experience with Brother Bell was miraculous, providential, or coincidental, I will never take lightly the matter of "spiritual feeding" or "caring for the lambs."

Do you have experiences that might be called "Biblical deja vu"? You remember a Biblical event or teaching, see something like it happening again, and think "This is just like what happened to ___ ___!" First of all, you need a working knowledge of the Scriptures for such similarities to impress you. Or you can recall the incident later as you are learning the Scriptures. You shouldn't be surprised, because life does tend to be cyclical; a lot of the same things happen again and again. Also, it can be comforting to see that the lives of Biblical people are not really that different from your own. For many of us, this is what makes our study of Simon Peter so stimulating. Like it or not, many of us are so much like him in so many ways. So if that's the case, we better try to learn from him!

Yes, the Lord was restoring Simon Peter, but it was than just re-establishing the relationship. He had things for Simon Peter to do – great things, like "Feed my sheep." When you are restored after some spiritual tumble, it's not only important to have the relationship with the Lord be made right, but also expect there to be immediate opportunities to resume your personal service to Him.

"Be shepherds of God's flock that is under your care" (1st Peter 5:2).

c. What About Him?

READ **John 21:18-23**

How are you doing with the inevitability of your getting older? Some seem to glide from one milestone to another (30th birthday, 40th birthday, 50th birthday, etc.) gracefully. Others seem to go kicking and screaming into older age. We all know factually of the reality, yea, the necessity, of this process. But accepting it emotionally is another thing! Christians should be the best at accepting this reality. Being older should bring greater faith and maturity in the Lord. Plus we have the happy prospect of graduating from this life to a better one in Heaven.

Aging is inevitable. But how would you like to have specific prophecies about how you would age and how you would die? When graduating from high school, most people probably give little thought to what they will be doing, how they will look, or where they will be in say, thirty years.

Simon Peter was given a look, at least generally, into his future. The one doing the prophesying is no one less than Jesus Christ Himself. And the view is not particularly promising! First, Jesus states that the apostle will, in fact, live to old age. Then He seems to indicate some kind of limitation or feebleness. Simon Peter won't be able to dress himself and direct his own steps as when he was younger. And finally the Lord indicates a kind of death, although undesirable, which would nonetheless glorify God. Jesus concludes this stunning look into the future with the solemn charge, "Follow me!"

When you think about it, although none of us will have this kind of specific prophecy from the lips of Jesus, our plight will be much the same. We will continue to grow older. As we age we won't enjoy all the youthfulness we once had. Unless we are living when Jesus returns, we will go through the process of physical death. It might be a sudden, untimely death. Perhaps we will struggle with a disease that will eventually take our life. Or we may simply die of old age. Whichever the case, we would certainly hope our death, like our life up that point, would glorify God. And most of all, whenever our life will end, we want to have continued to faithfully follow Christ all the way.

This new information, immediately following the questions about love from Jesus, must have been too much for Simon Peter to bear. He needs to deflect some attention. You know about deflecting, don't you? We all do it. Children master it very quickly.

It's prompted by desire to change the subject when whatever is happening is hitting too close to home.

So Simon Peter turns to John. This is the John who wrote the gospel account, which we know by the same name. In it he refers to himself several times as "the disciple whom Jesus loved." This is not to suggest he was the only one loved by the Lord. It does perhaps imply John was Jesus' closest friend on earth, a fact seemingly borne out in various ways from Scripture. Simon Peter's question "Lord, what about him?" seems to be asking, "How and when is he going to die?"

Jesus twice makes the point if He wants John to stay alive until He returns, what is that to Simon Peter? In other words, "Don't worry about him; worry about what I asked you to do – follow me!" This conversation gave rise to a rumor that Jesus said John would not die. The text specifies that that isn't what Jesus said and reiterates the point that it's Jesus business if he wants to keep John alive until He returns. History indicates John lived a long time, perhaps almost to the end of the first century. But he died, and Jesus has not yet returned.

I have a lot of quirks in my life, but fear of dying is not one of them. Thanks to some good teaching I received early in my own discipleship training, I accepted death as a part of life. I have accepted the fact than when I die is not nearly as important as how I die, that is, faithful to Christ.

I did, while my children were being raised, ask the Lord many times to spare my life until they were on their own. That time has come and passed. I still have lots of things I want to do for Christ on this earth, but I've stopped asking God to honor any timetables.

For my 50th birthday, my wife and kids gave me a special gift – an opportunity to do something I had dreamed of doing for decades: I went skydiving! Some of my friends concluded I must have a death wish. Not so! While many wouldn't even consider such a thing, for me it was a real thrill, and I didn't think I was a daredevil at all. I think I take a bigger chance every time I drive my car.

While I probably won't go skydiving again, I want to keep facing challenges in my life as long as I am physically, mentally, and emotionally able. I love life and want to live it to the full! And I'm not going to spend a lot of time or energy worrying about death. Thanks to my relationship with God through Christ, that's all taken care of!

Have you made peace with the inevitability of your own aging process and dying? If you haven't done this, please consider working on it – as soon as you can, and as seriously as you can. Your witness will not be as strong if you are living under clouds of doubt and fear about these realities of life. The book of Philippians offers an especially good study on this subject.

"As long as I live in the tent of this body, because I know that I will soon put it aside, as our Lord Jesus Christ has made clear to me." (2nd Peter 1:13,14)

d. Simon Peter Uses "The Keys" For the First Time

READ Acts 2:14-41

If there was any doubt the Lord intended for Simon Peter to be fully reinstated into God's plan, it was settled by the principal role the apostle played in the events of the Day of Pentecost. This was one of the major Jewish festivals, actually a celebration of the harvest of wheat, held 50 days after the Passover Feast. For Simon Peter, this may have been the high-water mark of his ministry. This is not to downplay the significance of any of the events leading up to this or discredit all that's going to transpire in the years that follow. It's just that this is the defining moment.

Simon Peter and the other apostles knew something was going to happen, but may not have realized its importance until some time later. Just ten days earlier they had stood gazing skyward as Jesus ascended from the earth. He had given them a commission to evangelize the world. And he had told them to wait in Jerusalem until they would "be clothed with power from on high" (Luke 24:49). So they had waited, and waited, and waited. You know the feeling when you are expecting something important to happen, but you don't know exactly what or when it will be. After ten days, they were probably about waited out!

Suddenly things did start happening: incredible things, unbelievable things, awe-inspiring things. This is the day the church of the Lord is to begin! Jesus had promised, "I will build my church" (Matthew 16:17). But even before Jesus began his public ministry, John the Baptist had prophesied about a time when the Spirit would be poured out on some of his followers, which included some of those who had become apostles. All of the lessons learned from Jesus pointed toward this day. This is the day that the New Covenant, prophesied centuries before, and referred to by Jesus as he instituted the Lord's Supper, is going to come into being. All references to "the kingdom" up to this point have been looking toward its establishment. All references hereafter in the New Testament will refer to its existence in the present tense. This is the big day!

This will be the beginning of what Jesus was talking about when he promised "the keys of the kingdom of heaven" to Simon Peter and the other apostles. What they "bind" and "loose" through their preaching and teaching will be "bound" and "loosed" as the true doctrine of the church for as long as it shall exist.

The Holy Spirit comes upon the apostles in a most dramatic fashion. This draws a crowd. Because of the religious festival, Jews from many countries are in Jerusalem. Amazingly, the apostles are speaking to these visitors in the languages of their respective countries. These ordinary, uneducated men are speaking in languages they've never studied!

Cynical observers try to dismiss the event with the absurd charge that the apostles are drunk. (Who would seriously think being drunk would make you proficient at speaking a variety of languages?) Simon Peter, with the other apostles standing around him, begins the sermon of his life. There would be other great sermons, for sure. But none would ever be as crucial, or receive such a response as this one.

In a word, the sermon was incredible. (If you didn't do so, please go back now and read Acts 2:14-40 – it won't take you long.) Simon Peter succinctly moves from dismissing the ridiculous charge about being drunk to the promise of the Spirit, the lineage of Christ, and the dramatic climax of the sermon. As the sermon reaches its crescendo, the apostle clearly points the finger of guilt to these listeners. They may have not participated in the scourging He received, or driven the nails into His hands and feet, but they are guilty. And this very One, whom they had crucified, this is the One whom God has declared to be both "Lord" and "Christ" (Messiah). This message struck to their very hearts!

There's an appeal from honest hearts: "What shall we do?" Simon Peter tells these who are very much displaying their belief to repent (commit to change) and be baptized in Jesus' name. The two immediate spiritual blessings will be the forgiveness of sins and the gift of the Holy Spirit. He continues to exhort (warn and plead) with many other words. The response is phenomenal!

When I get to Heaven, if such things are allowed, I would love to see a replay of this dramatic event. I'd love to see how Simon Peter delivered these incredible words and at the same time watch the faces of the people as the message began to sink in. Then it would be thrilling to watch as people responded to this first sermon in the church age.

I have been privileged to baptize many people, but usually only one or two at a time. Every time I've done this, I've felt privileged to do so and genuinely thrilled. Frankly, I can't begin to imagine how Simon Peter and the other apostles must have felt, baptizing about 3,000 people that day!

In thinking about Simon Peter's involvement in this momentous day, I'm reminded of an old country saying "Who woulda thunk it!" Imagine going to this man five years earlier, before he met Jesus, even before the ministry of John the Baptist. He would be Simon, not yet nicknamed Peter. He would be in the midst of building his career as a young fisherman. And imagine saying "Simon, on the Day of Pentecost five years from now, you'll stand before a multitude in Jerusalem and deliver a sermon that will be remembered for all time. Thousands will respond to your message, committing themselves to a new religion, of which you will be a leading spokesman for some time." He would have probably looked at you and said something like "You're crazy!"

Study the sermon Simon Peter gave that day. Incorporate its truths into your whole understanding of the gospel. And then faithfully proclaim that message, with all it requires of those who receive it, for as long as you possibly can.

"Praise be to the God and Father of our Lord Jesus Christ! In his great mercy he has given us new birth into a living hope through the resurrection of Jesus Christ from the dead" (1st Peter 1:3)

PRINCIPLE TEN

"Hang in Long Enough and You'll Begin to Succeed"

a. What I Have, I Give You

READ **Acts 3:1-26**

This chapter tells of Simon Peter's second great sermon. The sermon itself is a great Christology. It is rich in doctrine and logic, especially in proclaiming Jesus as the fulfillment of Old Testament prophecy.

But it all started with an interesting incident involving a crippled man, a beggar. The beggar, as he did with so many others entering the temple courts, had asked Simon Peter and John for money. What he ended up getting was a lot more than a few coins to add to his purse: he received healing, and it seems safe to assume a new relationship with God.

There are some intriguing elements in this story. The first is how Simon Peter immediately responds to the question – he looks straight at him, as does John. (Do you remember at the outset of the book, when you were asked to remember how Jesus looked at Simon before He gave him his new name of Peter?) While we don't know the full meaning of this, it is surely a good practice to actually go ahead and look at people when they are asking you a question. (Have you noticed how in our largely impersonal society, many have trouble making eye contact with another person?) Second, in what seems to be a rather demanding way, Simon Peter tells the man, "Look at us!" Again, we're only left to wonder the full meaning of this. Perhaps the man was only asking for help in a mechanical, sing-song kind of way, not really wanting to be too much of a bother and perhaps not expecting much from his appeals. While we have to be careful not to be too demanding, if people engage us in conversation, for whatever reason, it's not wrong to hope they'll pay attention to our response. In any case, the apostles' response does get the man's attention. He was expecting a handout, but received something else.

Simon Peter explains he has no money, but quickly offers something much more valuable – healing from his crippled condition. In the midst of the dialogue is a most compelling phrase (Did you catch it?): "What I have, I give you."

Wouldn't you love to have the power and ability possessed by these apostles? You see a physical need, and you instantly address it. But, alas, there are no apostles around today to do these kinds of miracles, or to lay their hands on any of us so we can. But this doesn't mean we still don't have much to give to people in need. Sometimes what people are asking for is not really their greatest need. If they will receive it, we Christians can give them loving attention, compassion, and a message of hope.

Being a beggar was and is an accepted way of life in some eastern and middle eastern societies. Not so in America! It is more tolerated than accepted, and by some folks it is not even tolerated. In this country, with its Protestant work ethic and the pull-yourself-up-by-your-own bootstraps mentality, some view beggars with disdain, especially if there's no physical malady easily detectable. To say the least, the beggar in our society would probably have a low degree of self-esteem. They probably receive many more derisive comments and glances than gifts or compassionate words.

Contemporary Christians are put in a tough spot with beggars. Many local governments post signs telling us not to give money to panhandlers. We struggle with doubts about whether or not they are simply lazy. At the same time we read the words of Jesus: "give to everyone who asks of you" (Matthew 5:42). Some argue these words from our Lord pertain to those with whom you have a relationship, not some wayward waif you randomly encounter. It's tough. Maybe you've dreamed of being a billionaire who could go into impoverished areas and hand out cash. But would that be the best thing to do? Or greater yet, wouldn't it be grand to encounter the lame, the blind, the mentally ill, and be able to instantly restore their health. What can we do? What should we do?

Perhaps one solution lies subtly hidden in our story. Give them what you have. Give them YOU – your attention, your compassion, and, if they'll receive it, the message of your faith. Jesus once said, "He who receives you receives me, and he who receives me receives the one who sent me" (Matthew 10:40).

I'm wide open for suggestions here! I have tried, unsuccessfully, in places like New York City, to engage beggars in conversation. I was willing to help them with a small amount of cash, but I wanted to talk with them as well. But more often than not it seemed they weren't willing to talk, and a few times I've been cussed out for asking them anything.

On occasional trips into Philadelphia, I ate at a certain fast-food restaurant that we didn't have where we lived. The restaurant is on a big street, but in a very rough part of town. I've hardly ever stopped there without being approached by someone asking for change so they could buy some food. Usually they told me how long it's been since they've eaten. I strongly suspected this money, if given, would go immediately to buy drugs or booze. But I didn't have the heart just to say no. So I invited them to come in with me so I could buy them a few hamburgers and a soft drink. I've never had a taker!

I've been given every excuse as to why they need the money to buy the food somewhere else. I usually end up saying something like "Look, if you're hungry I'll buy you a meal right here, but I'm not going to give you any money." I'm not telling these stories because it makes me glad I outwitted a street person. Every time it happens, it breaks my heart. I wish I could do more.

What I can do is be more attentive to the questions I am asked by people in less urgent situations. Notice I didn't say less important situations. While someone may not be physically hungry or trying to fund an addiction, they may be spiritually starving. Probably like you, I want to be able to relate to people in such a way as to help them address their deepest need – a right relationship with God through Jesus Christ.

If you've experienced the frustration described above, then join me in saying the following prayer: "Lord, please help me be a person interested in truly helping others. As is actually in their best interest, help me know when and how to share with the needy. But help me also, Lord, to always be willing to give what I have that's beyond money. In Jesus' name, Amen."

"Offer hospitality to one another without grumbling." (1st Peter 4:9)

b. The First Arrest

READ **Acts 4:1-20**

You knew it was going to happen sooner or later. You knew, that is, if you were paying attention to what Jesus had said during his ministry. He had clearly warned is disciples they would be arrested. It had to happen a first time, and this is it. Normally people are arrested for hurting or killing others, stealing or destroying property, or various crimes of dishonesty. With such arrests come varying degrees of shame and reproach. Not so here! Simon Peter and John are arrested for helping a man and using the occasion to share the message of Jesus.

This story has several interesting aspects you might not expect. For example, if this was supposed to have a dampening affect on the growth of the church, the strategy surely failed. Just after the text mentions their arrest, there is a statement about the phenomenal numerical growth of the church.

Also of special interest is the emphasis given on the name of Jesus. Jesus' name is specifically referred to five times in this relatively short section. From its occurrence here, as well as other writings from the same time period, we learn a name could imply authority. For example, if one came "In the name of the Emperor" that carried great significance. This becomes more meaningful when we remember we pray "in the name of Jesus." Although we won't fully address it here, it is important to remember that the proper use of the name of Jesus has real clout. We've seen in the movies where someone used someone's name to gain admittance where they otherwise wouldn't be allowed to go. Well, how about being allowed into the very throne room of God to speak to the Creator Himself! We can do that, you see, when we come to the Father "in the name of Jesus."

This is also the section where we find the phrase we've referenced several times, how the apostles were perceived as "unschooled, ordinary men." Those who viewed them in this way were "astonished," no doubt at the miracle they had performed, and probably more so at the courage they displayed.

In this incident we can't help but notice the development of Simon Peter. He's allowing the Holy Spirit to lead him in his speech. He's quoting Scripture. And, as we shall see later, he is even so bold as to openly challenge the religious leaders on the apostles' right to minister so boldly in the name of Jesus.

100

Finally, this is the place (Acts 4:12) where Simon Peter makes the statement that prompted a whole wave of "ONE WAY!" buttons, tee shirts, posters, and bumper stickers a generation ago. Declaring Jesus to be the only way to salvation and a right relationship with God is not culturally acceptable these days, but it's still true!

I've never been arrested, either for criminal or spiritual reasons. But I know some great servants of Christ who had many scrapes with the law before their conversion. Never having been in this kind of trouble is good on the one hand, but that alone would not necessarily indicate righteousness. Some who have never run afoul of the law would also never manifest enough conviction to be arrested because of their faith, if that were a possibility. (It reminds me of the old question, "If you were put on trial for being a Christian, would there be enough evidence to convict you?") I think it may be too easy for those of us who live in free societies to take our religious freedoms for granted. There are still plenty of places in the world where if you tried to share your faith in Jesus, you would be arrested immediately. I admire those who conduct fruitful ministries for Christ under such threatening circumstances. I remember hearing of the daring of some who, years ago, would sneak Bibles into countries behind the Iron Curtain. God may lead me someday to one of those hard fields where arrest and harsh punishment are a part of the cost of discipleship. Meanwhile, I want to be an everyday freedom fighter – both appreciating and advocating the religious freedoms I enjoy, and trying to influence those I can to find spiritual freedom in Christ.

As a citizen of this world, conduct your daily life in such a way that criminal arrest isn't a worry. As a citizen of the Kingdom of God, conduct your life with the awareness the world will, to varying degrees, hate Jesus' disciples just as they hated Him. Don't seek persecution or martyrdom. But if in the process of being faithful to Christ either happens, accept them as part of the glory of serving Christ.

"If you are insulted because of the name of Christ, you are blessed, for the Spirit of glory and of God rests on you. If you suffer, it should not be as a murderer or thief or any other kind of criminal, or even as a meddler." (1st Peter 4:14,15)

c. Simon Peter, the Prosecuting Attorney

READ **Acts 5:1-11**

When we read some Bible stories, we just have to trust the sovereignty of God! We must believe He has the ability to make the right decisions and take the right actions, even if we don't fully understand. This kind of faith is not attainable with a limited knowledge of God. The more we know about God – and this comes only from sustained and serious study of His Word – the more we are able to accept His judgments and responses.

God's sovereignty is very much at play in this story. He makes a decision to discipline two people in the most severe of ways, punishment by death. In so doing, He not only removes these two deceitful people from the immediate context of the local church, but also deeply impresses the church, both then and now, of His disdain for sin.

In this instance we have to accept He knew more than we could ever know of what was going on in the two people's hearts, what they would or wouldn't have done in the future to correct it, and how this type of sin would affect the church. Just because God doesn't deal as instantaneously with sin in the church today as He did on this occasion, we must not view His forbearance as license. God's judgment today is usually not as sudden, but it will be, in the end, just as certain!

If the story of Annanias and Sapphira strikes great fear in you as it did in the whole church in Jerusalem, then learn the obvious lesson. As soon as you are aware you have sinned, move quickly to repent. Confess it at least to God and if it's publicly known, confess it to the whole church and seek their prayers (see Acts 8:22-24 and James 5:16). Trust in God's promise to forgive your sins when you confess (1 John 1:9). Resolve to put that particular sin behind you (see John 8:11). Whatever you do, don't run the foolish risk of thinking, "I'll take care of that someday." Someday may never come.

For our purposes, we are intrigued to see Simon Peter being used, in effect, as the prosecuting attorney in this matter. The apostle is called upon to ask the hard questions and draw the condemning conclusions. Although it doesn't say so in the text, we trust that Simon Peter was acting in this situation under the direct guidance of the Holy Spirit.

Contemporary church leaders are never put in such a position where immediate death is going to be the outcome of one's sin being exposed. However, church leaders are called upon at times to lead

102

the church in the painful but necessary process of church discipline (see Matthew 18:15-18; I Corinthians chapter 5). These actions are never to be done for the purpose of punishment – that is exclusively God's domain. They are done in the hope of restoring an erring one to a right relationship with God.

At those times when we have to decide whether or not to continue to have fellowship with a fellow Christian who is trapped in sin, we must do so with the greatest caution and care. First, we must be certain the person's actions are clearly in contradiction to what the Bible says is right. There is no room for personal opinions or preferences – their actions must be indisputably wrong according to the Bible. Secondly, our attempts to restore such a one must be done in the absolute spirit of Christ (see Galatians 6:1-5).

Over the years I've been in a few situations where a congregation was reluctantly forced to engage the New Testament practice of church discipline already mentioned. Even when this action is unquestionably warranted and you're glad the congregation has the faith to do it the Biblical way, it is still quite disconcerting. Sometimes these efforts have succeeded; sometimes they have not. But these experiences have left me with two abiding convictions. I don't want to live my life in such a way as to cause a local church to take this action toward me. And ultimately, I want to be a joyful recipient of God's gracious welcome into Heaven, not a disheartened recipient of His wrath.

Just like many people institute a self-improvement program to address any number of personal deficiencies, why don't you institute a spiritual growth program to insure your relationship with Christ? If you make a point of seeking spiritual growth every day of your life, which includes addressing sins as they occur, then you most surely won't find yourself in a position of being disciplined, either by God or the church.

"Therefore, my brothers, be all the more eager to make your calling and election sure. For if you do these things, you will never fall, and you will receive a rich welcome into the eternal kingdom of our Lord and Savior Jesus Christ." (2nd Peter 1:10-11)

d. Power in His Shadow!

READ Acts 5:12-16

Sometimes we have to freely admit we do not understand all the marvels and mysteries of certain Biblical stories. This story is a good case in point. The overall emphasis seems to be on how God is miraculously working through the apostles, and Simon Peter in particular, mightily confirming this new message and church.

But people being healed merely by having someone's shadow fall on them – wow! We've grown somewhat accustomed to miraculous healing by Jesus, and later the apostles. People's health was restored by a touch or spoken words. But this adds whole new dimensions for our consideration. First, God's power can be manifested in ways we would never imagine. Second, Simon Peter seems to be especially empowered in this regard. We can only surmise that if he were in fact filling some kind of ex officio role as leader of the apostles, the people would recognize the greatest miracle-performing abilities in him.

This almost unbelievable power reminds us of "extraordinary miracles" by Paul mentioned in Acts 19:11. "Extraordinary miracles" seems almost redundant, don't you think? On the face of it, all miracles are "extraordinary." In our vernacular we'd probably describe these "extraordinary miracles" with a phrase something like "super-miracles." In the situation involving Paul, clothes or handkerchiefs that had touched his body were carried to others for healing or to cast out evil spirits.

While we read with awe these great apostolic feats, it reminds us also of the copycat antics of religious frauds throughout the Christian era. (There's another whole subject of study regarding miracles in which we shall not engage here.) Even in the recent past we have seen the overt commercialization of supposed healers, complete with their "prayer cloths" that for the right price will supposedly provide healing and other spiritual blessings.

What we will engage in is observing how God worked so incredibly through these ordinary men. While the manifestations are not as dramatic today, He still does great things through ordinary men and women and boys and girls who love Him, and are willing to simply serve in His name.

Many younger people might not consider ministry to the sick as fun or cool as other ministries. Youthful Christians might tend to say, "Ministries like singing, youth ministry, camp work, and even soul winning, those are all valid ministries. But ministering among the ill? I mean that's depressing. Those people are not fun to be with; many of them are dying!" What I'm describing is the attitude I had when I was a youth minister, in my mid-twenties. Fortunately that began to change under the tutelage of the late Doug Lawyer, the preacher where I was working at that time. Doug is one of my greatest heroes, and one of the very best friends I ever had. Visiting the sick in our large congregation was not one of the duties on my job description. But somehow Doug must have sensed I desperately needed some training in this area, and, more importantly, the compassion to go with it. So two or three times a week, when he was making his visits to the hospitals, nursing homes, or to shut-ins at home, he would insist I go along. I liked being with Doug, so I went. What I now realize is how this began to change my perspective on ministering to those who are suffering, or bereaved, or lonely. An amazing thing was being planted in my heart. Before, I had not appreciated this phase of ministry; in fact I almost resented it! But now I was developing an awareness of its helpfulness to those in need. The germination continued, even after I had moved on to another ministry and saw Doug only occasionally. Years later it dawned on me that visiting people in their suffering is one of the best things I get to do as a minister. Even now, more than 30 years after our work together, and several years after his death, I still use Doug's technique when visiting the sick. I hear myself using some of his expressions in the prayer I say before I leave the hospital room. I even hear myself using some of the same friendly banter (corny jokes!) used by my dear friend, and discipler, brother Doug.

Did you know we can all be doctors, of a sort, when we speak or teach or preach the words of God to others? Scripture encourages us to be "sound" in our doctrine (Titus 2:1). That soundness means a whole lot more than just expressing what's been traditionally accepted in your church fellowship. The word sound is a synonym for healthy. (Last wills and testaments often read, "Being of sound mind and body.") When you faithfully speak the words of God, you are dispensing healing words. When and how God heals physical disease is His business. Being messengers of the healing words of the gospel is the business (assignment) He's given us. This can be done through preaching and teaching, but it's also done in the everyday conversations that occur in car rides, on coffee breaks, and across the backyard fence.

"... by his wounds you have been healed." (1st Peter 2:24)

105

PRINCIPLE ELEVEN

"Never Assume You've Grown Enough"

a. Simon Peter on the Subject of Obedience

READ **Acts 5:29-32**

Obedience is neither a word nor a concept to which we are naturally drawn. Nowhere else do we so easily see the conflict between our natural man (includes both men and women) and the spiritual man God wants us to be. We don't want to obey; we want to give orders! Advertising slogans, popular songs, and even TV and movies tell us we can and should expect to have it our way. Those who study social trends dubbed the 1980s as the "me decade." Nothing's really changed in this regard since then!

Since the beginning of time, selfishness has been at the very heart of mankind's problems. And selfishness does not peaceably coexist with obedience. A simple definition of obedience implies one has to either willingly or under duress depart from self-direction to follow the direction of another or others.

Do you want an example of how we're prone to react negatively to the idea of obedience? Just mention "obedience school" and most folks will say "That's for dogs!" But to become the men and women God wants us to be for service in His Kingdom, all of us will have to enroll, as it were, in His "obedience school."

When one seriously begins the process of learning to obey God, they have turned the corner in life that will, both immediately and eventually, set them apart from normal human thinking and behavior. Unfortunately, many never dare to venture into this realm. It is very easy, sometimes even commended, in the world's system to go through life resisting, in ways both great and small, any kind of obedience.

As an impetuous person Simon Peter no doubt found (as many of us find today) obedience a most galling concept. We have already seen in episode after episode how his way of thinking and acting had to be brought into compliance with the Lord's. So by the time we come to this incident, Simon Peter has already spent a lot of time in the "school of obedience" directed by the Lord Jesus Christ. It was upon this basis he was well prepared to speak to anyone, including here his persecutors, on the principle of obeying God.

If we didn't know better, from this story we'd think Simon Peter and the other apostles were brilliant lawyers. (We'll give the Holy Spirit a lot of the credit!) In Acts 4:19 they had raised a rhetorical point regarding obedience to which the religious leaders had no comeback. Now in 5:29 they emphatically answer their own question: "We must obey God rather than men!" Notice also in verse 32 their mention of how those "who obey him" are given the Holy Spirit.

If you wish to feel better about the matter of obedience, remember in the Bible the words faith and obedience are practically synonymous. But somehow seems easier to aspire to greater faith than to greater obedience! We sing the words "trust and obey, for there's no other way, to be happy in Jesus, but to trust and obey." The connection between faith and obedience is one of the recurring themes of the Old Testament. Jesus stated it in John 3:36 (see especially in the RSV). Three times in the book of Romans (nicknamed "the epistle of faith") Paul shows the inexorable link between faith and obedience. (See Romans 1:5, 6:16-18, 16:26.) James, without using the word obedience, nonetheless drives home in his book the relationship between faith (believing in something) and works (doing something). Simon Peter will mention some form of the word obedience several times in his two short letters.

After my own baptism into Christ a number of people kept congratulating me with a phrase with which I was unfamiliar. They kept saying, "We're so glad you 'obeyed the gospel.'" What I soon discovered is the phrase "obeying the gospel" (which is not well known to many) is in the Bible. Some form of "obey the gospel" can be found at Romans 10:16 (KJV, RSV), 2 Thessalonians 1:8, and 1 Peter 4:17. Now the phrase "obey the gospel" is one of my very favorites. I like to both encourage people to do it or congratulate them when they have done it. The phrase itself so beautifully describes how one puts their faith into action (obedience) as they hear and respond to God in the plan of salvation He has given in His Word.

If you've always been a person who has found it difficult to obey – your parents, teachers, traffic laws, etc. – then learning to obey God will be a great challenge. But as you persevere in this regard, this can be one of the most dramatic and rewarding areas of your conversion to Christ. Remember it won't happen overnight, just like it didn't happen for Simon Peter overnight. But it must happen if you are going to keep moving toward maturity in Christ.

"For it is time for judgment to begin with the family of God; and if it begins with us, what will the outcome be for those who do not obey the gospel of God?" (1st Peter 4:17)

108

b. Simon Peter the Missionary

READ **Acts 8:1b-25**

If you know much about the apostles you probably already think of all of them as missionaries. But they were reluctant missionaries, in spite of all their training and specific directions from the Lord Jesus.

As stated previously, the word missionary does not occur in our English Bibles. In the original Greek the word apostle means "one sent." This passage reminds us of an earlier time when Jesus, in the midst of His earthly ministry, sent His newly appointed apostles out on their first preaching tour. Later, before His ascension into Heaven, Jesus said they were to go "into all the world" (Mark 16:15). Our word missionary is actually something of an anglicization of the Latin word for apostle.

Before His departure Jesus had given the apostles specific directions as to how they were to spread the gospel, a geographic strategy if you will. In Acts 1:8 He had told them they would be His witnesses "in Jerusalem, and in all Judea and Samaria, and the ends of the earth." Think of the circles that move away from where a rock hits the water in a pond. Starting from their home base (Jerusalem), they were to move into the surrounding region (Judea and Samaria) and eventually on outward to the farthest known parts of the world. This was a logical plan, but the apostles hadn't followed it.

The new church experienced phenomenal spiritual and numerical growth in Jerusalem, even with opposition by the ruling Jewish leaders. And it seems the apostles and others, probably without intending to, had become quite comfortable in their ministries there. All that was going to dramatically change, through something Jesus had specifically predicted – persecution.

Immediately following the stoning of Stephen (Acts chapter 7), a great persecution against the church scattered many in the church to Judea and Samaria – the exact area Jesus said they were to go next! The apostles were not included in this scattering. As the Christians were scattered, they preached the message wherever they went. Samaria was especially responsive to the good news, and it wasn't long before the apostles needed to send reinforcements to assist in the various challenges produced by such dramatic growth. They sent Simon Peter and John. So this was the first of many times the apostles would travel, finally becoming true missionaries to the world. We don't know if all the apostles traveled as much as

Simon Peter and later Paul, but the exploits of those two make up much of the rest of the book of Acts.

Back to Samaria, an interesting "story within the story" involves Simon the Sorcerer (or magician). Previously he had bedazzled the folks thereabouts with his trickery. As the gospel was being so enthusiastically received, Simon the Sorcerer himself believed and was baptized. The text says he was impressed with the miracles being done by Philip – no doubt recognizing their genuineness as compared to the illusions he performed. A new dimension was realized when the apostles arrived, imparting miraculous manifestations of the Spirit through the laying on of their hands. When he realized the apostles possessed this remarkable ability, he tried to buy this ability for himself. This led to one of the sternest rebukes ever uttered by Simon Peter. He quite literally says that Simon the Sorcerer and his money will perish in perdition (Hell) for thinking the gift of God could be bought with money. He goes on to identify in Simon the Sorcerer a serious spiritual malady – the malady present whenever one is dangerously close to losing his place in the Kingdom. "Your heart is not right before God." Fortunately Simon the Sorcerer repents and asks for their prayers. Some have dubbed the principle introduced here as "the second law of pardon." When one has a sinful attitude and actions evident to all, they should repent and ask the church to pray for them. Sometimes this realization is brought to them by others; sometimes by their own conscience and knowledge of the truth. Once restored, a Christian can again enjoy the full blessings of a right relationship with God and His people.

On their return trip to Jerusalem, Simon Peter and John preached in many Samaritan villages. Hey, this "missionary work" wasn't so bad after all! They better get used to it, for it would be their primary activity for the rest of their lives.

I have had to publicly repent of sinful attitudes and actions. Although I wish it hadn't been necessary, after it was over I have always been glad I did it. It is always the right thing to do. I have counseled dozens of others, in similar situations, to do the same. Unlike some problems, sin will not just go away. It absolutely must be addressed privately between you and God, and if publicly known, then with those with whom you worship and serve, as well. Although much more serious, because of its eternal ramifications, dealing with sin in one's life is like having to remove a splinter. While it is painful at the moment, it will only get worse until it is addressed. (As silly as it might seem, I suppose an unattended splinter could get infected, and if never treated could eventually kill you.) Unattended sin is a much more serious problem. Don't be one who would bravely remove a splinter, or ask someone to do it, but never deal with a sin problem.

You can be a missionary without ever leaving your hometown. The Lord needs millions of ambassadors, even in a relatively evangelized country like the United States, sharing their faith in neighborhoods, workplaces, schools, community groups, and wherever else you encounter people. One way to be motivated and trained for every day mission work where you already live and work is to go on a mission trip where the gospel is not so well known. Many teens and adults have had their spiritual lives greatly enhanced through this kind of experience. More churches should devote resources to sending their members, especially teens, on mission trips. This investment will pay big dividends in a congregation's local outreach.

"To God's elect, strangers in the world, scattered throughout ... who have been chosen according to the foreknowledge of God the Father, by the sanctifying work of the Spirit, for obedience to Jesus Christ" (1st Peter 1:1-2).

c. Simon Peter Ministering Here And There

READ **Acts 9:32-43**

Once Simon Peter started traveling he couldn't seem to stop, as indicated by the phrase "As Peter traveled about the country." The latter part of Acts chapter 9 includes the stories of the healing of a paralytic and the raising of a servant-hearted woman from the dead. Other than introducing us to names of towns and people we otherwise wouldn't know, there is nothing remarkable (remarkable in this context of signs and wonders) about these occurrences, except for one thing. They seem so familiar, in a way, because they are so very much like some of the miracles performed by Jesus during his earthly ministry. We shouldn't be surprised, after all, to see these well-trained apostles carrying on their work in ways similar to their Master.

This may be a good occasion to revisit the whole idea of the ways in which our main character, Simon Peter, is perhaps so much like us, or vice-versa.

First is the simple but profound principle of getting started. You know those situations where you know what you need to do, and perhaps even how to do it, but you just can't bring yourself to get started. While we have no reason to think the apostles and other disciples were lollygagging around Jerusalem (they were busy!), yet it took something outside of themselves – persecution – to get them out into the mission field. There may be right now in your life any number of good things you know you should be doing – both spiritual and otherwise – but you are hesitating. It could be an exercise program, or a daily Bible reading program, or making a commitment to one of the ministries within your local church. What's it going to take to get you started? Let's hope it wouldn't have to be something dramatic or even tragic in your life. But if you don't self-start, that's what may have to occur for you to proceed. Scripture teaches us God doesn't cause all things to happen, but He can cause good to come from all things that happen. (See Romans 8:28).

The second principle of which we're reminded in these stories is the whole principle of discipling. Those who are successfully imitating their master (mentor, hero) will find themselves involved with the same types of opportunities and/or struggles in which their master was involved. So it's no surprise to see Simon Peter traveling from place to place, finding opportunities to do good, being summoned from one place to go and assist in another, and forging new relationships in the Lord with people all along the way. This is

112

exactly how Jesus spent so much of His time. Simon Peter and the other apostles are merely following suit.

There's one caution that should be sounded here. Obviously Simon Peter and the others, as they traveled about, were carrying out the express directions of the Lord. And therefore we believe the Lord provided them with the financial support they needed. While many of us would like to just take off on open-ended mission trips, we have to deal with the realities of resources for food, clothing, transportation, lodging, and perhaps caring for loved ones back home. So all of us non-apostles are somewhat constrained by the demands of jobs and other responsibilities. This doesn't mean, though, we shouldn't try to plan and save for special adventures of service and outreach in remote places. Wonderful opportunities for some involvement will regularly present themselves to one who is open for such.

With this mention of discipling, I should point out I have been blessed with having a large number of role models for my training in ministry. Some of these men I have mentioned already in the book; for the others this will be the only mention of their name. It is difficult to both start and conclude such a list. While I have been richly blessed through association with many wonderful men and women in Christ, these stand out as ones especially significant in my training for work in the Kingdom. They may or may not be known to you, but they are my heroes.

Jim Massey – missionary and College Bible teacher
K.C. Moser – College Bible teacher
Stanley Shipp – missionary and coworker
Landon Saunders – seminar speaker, preacher
Don Flatt – professor, preacher, author
Doug Lawyer – missionary, preacher, and coworker
Jay Lockhart – preacher and coworker
Don Garrett – elder

Did the section on getting started perhaps prick your conscience just a little? They say good preaching comforts the afflicted and afflicts the comfortable! Maybe these words have done the same. Just remember: God has never given a command to anyone that was impossible to carry out. Not all of his commands may pertain to you in your particular situation, but some of them do. You probably have more resources for motivation at your disposal than you realize: the Scriptures, the Holy Spirit, prayer, trusted Christian friends, godly church leaders, and your local congregation as a whole. Find the encouragement, then go ahead and get started doing what you know the Lord wants you to be doing.

"Young men, in the same way be submissive to those who are older." (1st Peter 5:5)

d. Another Lesson for Simon Peter to Learn

READ **Acts 10:1-23**

This story sets the stage for the exciting expansion of the gospel into the Gentile (non-Jewish) world. We are introduced to a God-fearing man who, along with his household, will be the first fully non-Jewish recipients of the good news of Jesus Christ. Cornelius, a man of importance, had a deep spiritual hunger and thirst. God chooses Simon Peter to be the messenger. But first the apostle needs to individually face an issue, which shall be a struggle for the church for some time – racism. (Remember, Simon Peter and all the other apostles, like Jesus Himself, were of Jewish ancestry. Although they've moved into Christianity, the apostles are, culturally at least, still Jews.)

Anger and resentment between Jews and Gentiles had been going on for nearly two thousand years. The Jews considered the Gentiles as pagans or heathens. The Gentiles considered the Jews as religious elitists. (Sounds somewhat like the animosity and suspicion that exists today between many religious and non-religious folks.)

Simon Peter is on a rooftop praying, and as he was hungrily awaiting the noonday meal, he falls into a trance. What ensues is fascinating! In a vision from the Lord, three times Simon Peter is encouraged to eat various animals which for some reason or another didn't fit his kosher diet. While Simon Peter is wondering about the meaning of the vision, he is assured by the Spirit to welcome and willingly go with the envoys that were about to arrive. Simon Peter welcomes the men as his guests, and the next day travels with them toward Joppa for the encounter with Cornelius and the others.

We understand God was stretching Simon Peter's thinking beyond where it had previously ventured. The lesson about accepting foods he considers unclean is really a lesson about accepting people he previously considered unclean. And we can appreciate the faith of Simon Peter, who with the Spirit's bidding, warmly welcomes those sent from Cornelius and eventually goes with them to share the message of Christ.

We all have prejudices to overcome. And we, as Christians, must learn to overcome our worldly tendency to develop and hold on to prejudices in the first place.

It just occurred to me that you might have no way of knowing my race. Does it matter? Would whatever I am racially make my writing any more or less meaningful? It shouldn't! But just so the following story makes sense, I'm white.

I grew up in the segregated south, prior to and during the Civil Rights Movement. I had no real reason to be prejudiced. I had grown up doing farm work and playing with black kids who lived nearby. Although I never saw anything akin to the hatred of KKK activities, I constantly heard racial slurs and jokes. It just seemed easier to be prejudiced against blacks than to think through the meaning of the whole thing. It was just what you were expected to do.

One particularly affable young black man, George, had endeared himself first to my grandfather, then the whole family, as a hard and honest worker. He was a natural athlete, a few years older than I. He attended the special (segregated) school for blacks in town. But instead of staying after school for sports activities, he had to come home and work to help his impoverished family. Nonetheless, he gave me my first serious competition on the basketball court.

Later, our schools were integrated, and others and I accepted, without incident, the newcomers to school and eventually one black player onto our basketball team. I had no problems with this, on the outside at least, but inside me the prejudice (which is insidious) still lurked.

Then there was college basketball, where I was suddenly on a team with more blacks than whites. For some reason the black ballplayers were especially gracious to me and took on the challenge of trying to give me a little "soul" training. (They joked I was the "whitest" guy they had ever seen!) So I got an education in black culture, was taught some dance steps, and developed a love for Aretha Franklin recordings. Later on in college, when I became serious about my faith, I conducted Bible studies with some of my teammates, and baptized several of them, including a special black friend, Ed. While I taught him how to become a Christian, he taught me more about accepting people different than myself.

You see, God was stretching my thinking, just as he had for Simon Peter so long ago, and for so many since. With me, he did it through basketball. I could go on with many other stories of wonderful black individuals and families in churches where I've ministered, like the group of inner city black kids (all Christians) who adopted me as "Keitha Kunta," based upon a character from Alex Haley's "Roots."

Through each of these experiences and relationships, the prejudice began to slowly melt away. Just like He had done for Simon Peter, God was showing me over and over that what's precious to Him must become precious to me. I'm not perfect in this regard yet. But the more I learn about the whole plan of God, the more I see there's no room in it for racial prejudice.

116

Ask yourself if you think you can minister as effectively as the Father wants you to if you are holding on to various prejudices against people. If you know (can admit) your prejudice is wrong, then ask God to help you repent (change). If necessary, share your decision and new commitment with a trusted friend or minister.

"Live as free men, but do not use your freedom as a cover-up for evil; live as servants of God." (1st Peter 2:16)

PRINCIPLE TWELVE

"Be Prepared For Anything!"

a. Don't Worship Me!

READ **Acts 10:25-26**

When Simon Peter and Cornelius met, the Roman official fell down (bowed, humbled himself) and worshipped the apostle. Even though Cornelius' heart was full of appreciation and he was trying to show respect, Simon Peter did not let this go on, even for a brief time. His response is a classic! The text says Simon Peter lifted up Cornelius and said "Stand up; I too am a man." This reminds us of the time when Paul and Barnabas were praised as gods (Acts 14:11-18). Their response seems strange to us, but was actually quite typical of the way Jews of that day showed their passionate distaste for something with which they disagreed: they tore their clothes.

Simon Peter was well acquainted with bowing before one who was worthy. He had once thrown himself at the feet of Jesus (Luke 5:8). While traveling with the Master, he had seen others fall at Jesus' feet. He had also heard Jesus criticize religious leaders for wearing pretentious clothing, wanting to be called by special titles, and expecting special treatment (Matthew 23:5-9). Simon Peter knew full well that neither he nor any other mere man is deserving of such worship from a fellow human being.

Oh that today more understood this same principle, both in the giving and receiving of worshipful honor to religious leaders! Yes, while it is true all Christians are to "honor one another" (Romans 12:10), anything akin to worship from one person to another is entirely inconsistent with the New Testament's teaching and examples.

Many preachers probably have had some situation where someone idolized them in a way that probably wasn't for the best. Here's one from me. I have written short articles for *Power For Today*, a daily devotional booklet. Although the readership is large and nationwide, only occasionally will someone comment about seeing one of my articles. There is no pay, except for the joy of writing, and the hope that someone will be encouraged or strengthened by my words. However, once I got an unexpected phone call during breakfast. It was a Christian from another part of the state whom I occasionally see at various church programs. His ten-year-old grandson had read one of my articles and commented on it to his grandpa. The older man had said, "Well, I know Keith Hodges." Apparently the boy was enthralled with the idea of his grandpa knowing somebody famous, and had convinced my friend to call and ask for my autograph! I said okay, and for a moment it went to my head. Then later, thankfully, I was able to think more sensibly about the situation.

I wrote the lad, but was careful to emphasize the importance of his interest in spiritual things and his learning to find the special way he could serve God. I deliberately did not acknowledge anything about my having written the article or my being anybody special. I signed the letter, but had avoided the lure of just sending him my autograph. I was concerned not only for the boy, but also for my attitude in the matter. Let's hope he'll outgrow a childish fascination with knowing somebody famous. More importantly, I hope I outgrow any desire for acclaim. Jesus warned about loving the praise of men (John 12:43).

Simon Peter said in 1 Peter 2:15 we are to reverence (set apart) Jesus as Lord in our hearts. Let's follow the principle ascribed by Jesus when He said, "Render to Caesar that which is Caesar's, and to God that which is God's" (Matthew 22:21). In other words, give to humans what is appropriate for humans, but only give to God what is appropriate for God.

"Clothe yourselves with humility toward one another, because, 'God opposes the proud but gives grace to the humble'." (1st Peter 5:5)

b. Simon Peter Uses "The Keys" To Open The Way to Gentiles

READ **Acts 10:27-11:18**

This is the exciting story of the extension of the gospel to Gentiles (non-Jewish people). In Acts 8 the gospel was taken to Samaritans; they had a mixed heritage that included Jewish ancestry and a somewhat corrupted form of Judaism – but they could technically still be called Jews. Then in Acts 9 we see the conversion of the Ethiopian official (better known as the Ethiopian eunuch), a Gentile no doubt, but one who was a proselyte (convert) to Judaism. Now Simon Peter is handed (on a golden platter, it seems) the opportunity to share the good news of Jesus Christ with these who are unquestionably Gentile in every way.

You may recall how Simon Peter, along with the other apostles, was promised "the keys to the Kingdom." He first used those "keys" as he preached to Jews in Jerusalem on that first Day of Pentecost after Jesus' ascension, the first day of the new church age. Now we're going to see not only him using those same keys among the Gentiles, but the completion of a promise made by Jesus at the outset of His ministry.

The story is fascinating both in its simplicity and in its outcome. Cornelius has a large group assembled to hear the visiting apostle. Simon Peter gives a short, simple, and powerful message regarding the person and work of Jesus. Just as Peter seems to be getting really warmed up, the totally unexpected happens. The Holy Spirit is poured out on the Gentiles who had been listening to the message. This astonished the Jewish Christians who were accompanying Simon Peter. In chapter 11 we learn from Peter's own words how this was just like the pouring out of the Spirit on the apostles on the day of Pentecost (see Acts 2). Simon Peter cites the words of the Lord about John the Baptist baptizing with water, but Jesus would baptize with the Holy Spirit. This is also the dramatic fulfillment of a prophecy from hundreds of years earlier, when it was declared God would pour out His Spirit on all people (see Acts 2:17ff; Joel 2:28-32). The "all people" (or, "all flesh") aspect had been fulfilled in two steps. First, there was the special anointing of the Spirit on Jews (the apostles), on the Day of Pentecost. Now a special outpouring of the Spirit was being given to Gentiles (Cornelius and his household). It took something this dramatic to convince the Jews that God really did want Gentiles in the church!

This special baptism by the Spirit only occurs twice in the New Testament, and, as already stated, was for very specific purposes.

It was not a routine aspect of either the gospel being shared or received, either before or after this event. There was no pattern being established here, either for the early church or anyone today.

Not to be lost in the unique aspects of this conversion story is the majesty of Simon Peter's brief sermon. It is rich! He packs a lot of truth into just a few lines. In fact, there are expressions used here in the presentation of the gospel that are unique to the New Testament. As an example, what a rare nugget exists in the statement, "how God anointed Jesus of Nazareth with the Holy Spirit and power, and how he went around doing good and healing all who were under the power of the devil, because God was with him" (Acts 10:38). This stands as a classic example of how the Holy Spirit was leading Simon Peter and the other apostles, just as Jesus had promised during His ministry. (See John 14:26)

I'm trying to imagine the simultaneous thrill and nervousness as Simon Peter and the other Jewish believers ventured into this place to share the gospel with the Gentiles. The thrill was in the realization they were going "into all the world" just as Jesus had commanded. Not nervousness because they were fearful, but because of not knowing how they and their message would be received. Of course I've never been involved with an experience on the scale of this story. But I've been involved in situations where as a part of a small group of believers, we shared our faith with a much larger group of unbelievers. And you know what? Those "heathens" aren't always as bad as you might expect. In fact, sometimes you find their spiritual hunger and thirst to be downright refreshing!

Would you like to have in your evangelism repertoire something non-threatening to tell about Jesus? It might prove helpful in those situations where you fear a real apprehension in your listeners. Then try talking about "how Jesus went around doing good" (Acts 10:38). There's something very attractive and compelling about somebody who only tried to do good for people. Most people would like to meet somebody like that. You can help them meet the only one who ever did it perfectly. And at the same time, we should all strive to "go around doing good" for as many people as we can every day of our lives. We won't do it perfectly, but if we do it consistently it will be noticed, and it may open doors for the gospel.

"Live such good lives among the pagans that, though they accuse you of doing wrong, they may see your good deeds and glorify God on the day he visits us." (1st Peter 2:12)

c. Another Arrest, And a Miraculous Deliverance

READ **Acts 12:1-19**

Persecution again raises its ugly head against the church in Jerusalem. King Herod has James put to death. He was John's brother. They were the fishermen who were among the first called by Jesus to follow him. And he was a member of the inner circle of Simon Peter, James, and John, who were privy to so many of the most significant of the Lord's miracles and teachings.

When the ruthless King Herod saw how this won him favor among some, he had Simon Peter arrested, perhaps intending to have him executed as well. King Herod was as wicked as his uncle who had tried to have the infant Jesus killed several decades before. (If you wish to see how this tyrant met his ironic demise, read Acts 12:19b-25.)

The story that unfolds is both touching and amusing. Simon Peter is the subject of the story, but not necessarily the hero. The church, on the other hand, is heroic in its faith, even with its human foibles.

The church was praying earnestly on Simon Peter's behalf. After being rescued from his cell by an angel, Simon Peter more or less sleepwalks as he follows the angel past guards and through a gate that opened by itself! After the angel's departure the text says, "Peter came to himself." Up until that point he'd thought the whole thing was a vision or dream. As he regains his perspective, he gives thanks to God for his rescue. Then he makes his way to the place where he knows many in the church have gathered to pray. It's the house of Mary, the mother of John Mark. (This is the same Mark who would later write the second book in our New Testament, many think with input from Simon Peter.)

Next come the funny parts. First we are introduced to Rhoda. As Simon Peter knocks on the door, Rhoda goes to the door, hears his voice, and is so overjoyed she runs in to tell everyone – leaving Simon Peter outside! But stranger yet is that although they've been praying for him, no one on the inside seems willing to accept her story, saying, "It must be his ghost." Simon Peter keeps on knocking, and finally they let him in. Astonished that it's really him, they listen as he explains his release.

You may be thinking the church wasn't so heroic after all. Let's give them credit for having the faith to pray, even if they weren't quite ready to have their prayers answered so quickly.

Oh that more would pray earnestly and learn by experience to look for the answer!

There was one occasion when I felt more like I was in the first-century church than at any other time I can recall. We were involved in a church planting where the church was not strong. The small group got started by meeting in our home, but within a few months needed a larger place. We were all set to rent a storefront, but were waiting for a variance from the local zoning board. One of the members of the zoning board was a Jewish businessman with whom I had become acquainted at the local coffee shop. Several times over breakfast we had enjoyed some lively conversations about life, religion, and politics. Another member of the zoning board was the town's mayor. I had an appointment on a certain evening to meet with the zoning board to make our request. That day I received a call from the mayor, who asked if he could see me as soon as possible. I soon found myself in his office trying to answer some tough questions about our plans for the storefront. Finally he said, "Keith, I have to be honest with you – I don't think you've got a chance!" Naturally I was disappointed, but thanked him for talking with me. I went home and immediately began calling all of the members of our small congregation at their jobs or homes. We quickly arranged a special prayer meeting at our house for 6:00 P.M., with the zoning board meeting scheduled for 7:00. Everyone showed up and began praying earnestly.

I left the prayer meeting at 6:45, accompanied by one of the men of the congregation. The zoning board of seven men sat at tables in a horseshoe arrangement, with a little podium facing them. Two businesses (tax-paying concerns) were called, and I noticed they had lawyers to speak for them. Of course we would not be a tax-revenue business for the city, and I'm certainly not a lawyer. The businesses were both quickly shot down, their requests for variances solidly rejected. I thought, "What am I doing here?" Then I heard the clerk call "Keith Hodges and The Westwood Church," so I stepped up to the little podium. Although I was on the high school debate team, had played basketball in front of large crowds, and preached hundreds of sermons all over, I can never remember feeling more nervous. Because the clerk had stated the particulars of each of the two previous cases before the lawyers started speaking, I stood waiting for something similar to happen. Finally someone said, "Well, are you going to say anything?" I said, "Oh, yes." and began to speak. In about 45 seconds I had said about everything I knew to say. Then the mayor said, "Mr. Hodges was in my office today, and we discussed this proposal. Tell them, Keith, about...." So I answered.

And he said, "Tell them, Keith, about...." a few more times, and I answered each time. At that point my Jewish businessman friend spoke up and said, "I make a motion we accept his proposal as it is given." The mayor seconded the motion, and it passed unanimously. I walked out of that meeting pretty much in the same daze I suspect Simon Peter was in when he was released from the jail. We quickly returned home to find the group still praying. When I told them the good news, they could hardly believe it. But when it all soaked in there was great rejoicing.

When God releases you from some prison in your life (the bondage of your sins, a perilous situation, a roadblock for you or your congregation, etc.), there are two options. You can walk around in a daze, never fully appreciating what's happened, and therefore not being able to fully thank God. Or, "coming to yourself," you can get on with your work for the Lord. Get in the habit of doing the latter!

"Through these he has given us his very great and precious promises, so that through them you may participate in the divine nature and escape the corruption caused by evil desires." (2nd Peter 1:4)

d. Growth Is An Exciting Thing To See!

READ **Acts 15:6-11**

Through most of this book, we've been watching Simon Peter come from being the most annoying of characters to one of the most lovable of characters. But this was not an easy or quick transformation. He stumbled a lot. But with all of the stumbling, one has to appreciate he got up from every stumble. That is his most admirable trait – he never quit!

Most of us enjoy hearing about someone's success story. We especially like it when the underdog somehow wins. Jesus saw potential greatness in Simon Peter before anyone else even thought about looking for anything special. And that greatness came to fruition by Simon Peter's allowing God to work on him for a long time. Guess what? It's exactly the same for any of us!

Did you catch the subtle differences in this story of the matured Simon Peter, as compared to when he first started following Jesus? First, he didn't have to be the first one to speak. The text plainly says, "There had been much debate." We can't know for sure, but it almost seems Simon Peter may have let everybody else have their say, and then he spoke. And did you notice how through his brief testimony, it is God who gets all of the credit, even in the part where he's talking about his own involvement? And most touching, do you see his big ol' heart shining through with compassion for the Gentiles, and acknowledgment for the grace of God?

This brief speech is the last record of the spoken words of Simon Peter in Scripture. His two short letters would be written years later. And there were, no doubt, many more sermons and other talks, public and private, before his death. But how refreshing to see his last recorded remarks demonstrating such wisdom and grace. For one who seemingly couldn't help but noticeably interjecting himself into every situation, our last glimpse of him is of a dignified Christian leader. He had certainly become "the rock" (Peter, Cephas) Jesus had envisioned so many years before!

As one who has been called upon to preach funeral sermons, I've had family or friends of the recently departed tell me, with a great sense of satisfaction, beautiful stories of something loving or profound said by that person immediately prior to their death. Likewise, I've heard some awful stories of unloving, angry, or crude things said by some just prior to their deaths. Those less noble parting words often leave painful memories to be borne by the survivors

126

for years. Ideally, we'd all like to have the last thing anyone heard us say be worthy of honorable quotation.

Alben W. Barkley, the vice-president under Harry Truman, was from my native Western Kentucky. He was a personal friend of my great-grandfather, also a politician from that area. "The Veep," as he was called all over the country, was a great orator. On one occasion, he concluded a speech with the words "I would rather be a servant in the House of the Lord than to sit in the seats of the mighty." Then, with the applause of a large audience ringing in his ears, he dropped dead. Newspapers all over the country exclaimed the noble words, which were the last in a life of service to his nation.

I have grandiose notions of drawing my last breath just after delivering a stirring sermon, or perhaps sharing the gospel with an unsaved person, or making some profound statement upon my deathbed. But if my last expression will have been loving and kind, that will suffice.

The Apostle Paul wrote, "Let your conversation always be full of grace, seasoned with salt, so that you may know how to answer everyone" (Colossians 4:6). Isn't it grand that in Simon Peter's last recorded words, he was talking about God's grace! We well serve those around us, ourselves, and most of all God, by following that exhortation. And on those occasions where you would not be proud to have the words you just spoke be your final ones, move quickly to apologize.

"So then, dear friends, since you are looking forward to this, make every effort to be found spotless, blameless and at peace with him." (2nd Peter 3:14)

PRINCIPLE THIRTEEN

"Keep Striving, And Maturity Will Come"

a. Simon Peter Knew Something of Grace

READ **Acts 15:11**

Normally most Bible students think of Paul as the champion of grace, because of the many well-known passages he wrote on the subject. As compared to Paul, most of the other New Testament writers don't mention grace very often. This is not to say they didn't understand it or teach it. Paul wrote the majority of the letters in the New Testament, and it seems his role to expound on this subject more than others. However, you might be surprised to learn Simon Peter mentioned grace ten times in his two short letters, as well as in his statement here in Acts 15:11.

Simon Peter understood grace because it had been so frequently given to him by the Lord Jesus. We have seen over and over in this study how Simon Peter blew it, only to be forgiven and reinstated by the Lord. To be a constant recipient of grace and not appreciate it is always a senseless tragedy.

One can study grace at the factual level, and gain a certain appreciation of its importance. But to receive it personally – that's when it becomes real to most people. To recognize your actions have left you without any excuse, deserving the full consequences of your misdeeds, and then to be forgiven, it's unbelievable!

Unfortunately, some try to follow Christ without understanding grace. They think their efforts and achievements will merit entrance into the Kingdom and eternal life. They might even subconsciously be thinking, "God is really lucky to have me on His side!" To miss the principle of grace is to miss the whole point of Christianity.

May the stories in the Gospels strike us as more than just interesting narratives. Through Jesus' encounters with some very needy people – spiritually needy – we can begin to grasp our need for a savior as well. We need to see ourselves as the leper, the woman caught in the act of adultery, the sinful woman who washed Jesus' feet with her tears and wiped them dry with her hair, the blind and lame and demon-possessed. We need to see ourselves not as worthy candidates for God's blessing, but as "sheep without a shepherd." If we view our personal situation as anything other than hopeless, we will probably deal with Jesus as a teacher but not as a redeemer.

I am a debtor to God's grace. And I am also a debtor to the grace of my wife, children, parents, other family members, friends, and many brethren. It does not make me happy that I have to say this, but I am glad I can say it! We never need to take grace for granted. Dietrich Bonhoffer, the German theologian killed in one of Hitler's concentration camps, wrote a classic book entitled *The Cost of Discipleship.* In it he coined the phrase "cheap grace." We diminish grace, make it cheap when we either take it for granted, or use it as a license to sin, as some did in the early days of the church. (See Romans 6:1, 2).

One of my favorite quotes is from the Apostle Paul: "But by the grace of God I am what I am, and his grace to me was not without effect" (1 Corinthians 15:10). I'm convinced when one really understands grace it will motivate them to service and faithfulness like nothing else.

Grace is one of my favorite subjects when I give sermons or classes, especially if I am speaking to a group for the first time. This subject is always readily received, and I often notice something remarkable happening while I am preaching about grace. (Preachers will know what I'm talking about here.) Any time a message is really connecting or hitting home with the listeners, it usually gets very quiet and everyone seems riveted on the words being spoken. This is what happens when I speak about grace. People want to hear about grace! People need to hear about grace!

Do you understand God's grace in your life at the most personal levels of your consciousness? Are you compelled by the grace you've been given to be a better servant of God or are you compelled by something else? For example, a sense of guilt is necessary in order to be ready to receive grace. But guilt, of and within itself, will not last as a motivator for sustained service to God.

If you sense within yourself a lack of appreciation for God's grace, please consider doing a personal exercise based upon 1 Timothy 1:12-17. This is the Apostle Paul sharing how God's grace took him from his state of wretchedness to the work of ministry and apostleship. As you do the exercise, notice how Paul mentions some of his sinful actions. Then substitute your vilest deeds for the ones he mentions. Then notice how Paul rejoices in the fact he has been called to serve God in spite of his past actions. Likewise, consider the Christian tasks to which you've been called, though you are unworthy, by the mercy and grace of God.

"But grow in the grace and knowledge of our Lord and Savior Jesus Christ. To him be glory both now and forever! Amen." (2nd Peter 3:18)

b. Another Rebuke

READ **Galatians 2:11-16**

It's hard to imagine. Simon Peter has come so far. Yet at least one more rebuke is necessary. This time the Lord's spokesman was a fellow-apostle, Paul. We have seen how eloquently and correctly Simon Peter defended the rightful place of Gentile believers in the church (Acts 15). At the meeting since dubbed the "Jerusalem Conference," he said all are saved by grace, and not by keeping circumcision and other practices of the Old Testament Law.

Later Simon Peter comes to Antioch, known as "the cradle of the Gentile church," and Paul's base of operations. While there he had freely fellowshipped and ate with Gentiles. But when certain Jews arrived from Jerusalem, he ceased his warm association with the Gentiles in deference to these visitors. In other words, whether or not he intended to, his actions seemed hypocritical.

Let's give Simon Peter the benefit of the doubt, assuming he probably wasn't consciously or deliberately being hypocritical. He was probably trying to avoid strife. He may have been trying to be expedient in this situation. Today it is sometimes called "political correctness." While trying to honor one group of people, without intending to you can violate larger, more basic principles of right and good, common sense, or even doctrine.

We sometimes see this same kind of situation among Christians today. For example, when we visit Christians in another congregation, and especially in a different culture, they may have customs and traditions differing greatly from that with which we are accustomed. We'll have to be on our toes not to jump to conclusions that because these practices are unfamiliar to us, they are necessarily Biblically wrong. Or, sometimes when new Christians or even "prospective Christians" are being blended into the life of our congregation, they may bring practices and understanding that are, in fact, in contradiction to the Bible. In our desire to keep them or win them we cannot be so accommodating as to accept teachings or practices clearly inconsistent with the Bible.

In the situation at Antioch, Paul had worked too long and too hard to establish equal footing for the Gentiles in the Lord's church. This inconsistency by Simon Peter was not only wrong in principle, but could have been devastating in its effect. Paul "opposed him to his face, because he was wrong." In other words, he directly confronted Simon Peter about the matter. We're not given the details, but apparently Simon Peter received this rebuke and made the

131

necessary correction. We shall see in the next lesson how Simon Peter seemingly didn't hold a grudge toward Paul because of this incident.

This lesson teaches many things, but one of the most important is how none of us, even those who should be the most mature of Christian leaders, are exempt from making mistakes. Oh, we'd like to fancifully think someday we will stop sinning, but it won't happen. We can and should grow to where we are sinning less and less – but flawless living: it won't happen. Sin is deceitful, and pride is one of its best allies. We need to remain constantly open to the "nurture and admonition of the Lord," (Ephesians 6:4) no matter our age or how long we've been a Christian. The process of correction, rebuke, and admonition may come as we privately read the Bible, or listen to a sermon or class or to some fellow Christian.

I have, by necessity, been rebuked many times by fellow Christians. I never liked it. But usually sooner or later I realized it was a necessary part of my either growing up or making some correction. Let's face it: no one likes being corrected. The typical responses are anger and resentment, at least initially. There are so many interpersonal dynamics involved, and all of them can be a challenge. Sometimes men don't like being confronted by women, or vice-versa. Some older people don't want to hear any correction from a younger person, or vice-versa. And what if the person giving the rebuke just happens to not be one of your favorite people anyway? Or, what if they are one of your favorite people and it is doubly embarrassing that they are the one having to speak to you? What if the rebuke comes from someone you barely know, and you are thinking to yourself, "Where does the person come off correcting me?"

Then you have those situations where someone rebukes you for something inconsequential or something based on a misunderstanding on their part. I remember the lady who told me rather sternly my neckties were "too loud" to be worn in the pulpit. She was one of the quietest and sweetest ladies in the church and not normally a complainer. You just never know what little thing is eating away at someone. The style at that time was rather flamboyant, and she must have liked it when the preachers all wore dark suits, white shirts, and a plain dark tie. We talked about it, and I told her I wanted to "be all things to all men" (1 Corinthians 11:22). I assured her it was not my intention to draw attention to myself, but to wear clothes that struck some kind of balance with what other men and boys in the congregation were wearing. Finally, I told her I would closely follow the men who served as anchors on the nightly network newscasts (that is a true barometer of fashion!). She seemed pleased with that answer, and we became better friends than before.

Did you catch the secret of what made that example work out successfully? Fortunately in that situation I listened, and we talked. In similar situations I had not done as well, and relationships were strained, if not broken. Far too often many of us will not listen very long to a rebuke and then not talk with that person for a long time afterwards, or maybe never again. Listening well is hard work. Not enough people really listen to God, much less another person. We'll be better off when we listen to one another in the church, even when we're being rebuked.

Accept some simple facts. (1) You are not ever going to be a perfect Christian. (2) With God's help you can get better and better. (3) To get better and better, you'll have to recognize your shortcomings, and work at changing. (4) A part of that getting better may be through the corrective words of fellow Christians.

Even more difficult than receiving a rebuke is properly giving one. The best advice I know on this matter is given in Galatians 6:1-5. The emphasis of this and other relevant passages is not so much on the content of the rebuke (what you say), but on your attitude as you do it.

"Therefore, dear friends, since you already know this, be on your guard so that you may not be carried away by the error of lawless men and fall from your secure position." (2nd Peter 3:17)

c. Kind Words for Paul

READ **2 Peter 3:15-16**

When asked, "Who were the two most prominent apostles?" most Bible students know the answer: Simon Peter and Paul. Galatians 2:7-8 indicates Simon Peter's ministry was more to the circumcised (Jews), whereas Paul's ministry was more to the uncircumcised (Gentiles). But these areas of emphasis were not exclusive in any way! While Simon Peter first ministered exclusively among Jews, he was the one who introduced the gospel to Gentiles (Acts 10). From that point on he frequently worked among the Gentiles and and strongly defended their right to receive the gospel. Likewise, Paul started his ministry among Jews, but later visited and wrote to people primarily in the non-Jewish world. Paul's coworkers, traveling companions, and ministerial apprentices were an interesting mix of Jews and Gentiles.

Some have speculated as to whether or not Simon Peter and Paul were something like rivals, although the Scriptures never indicate such a nature to their relationship. From a human standpoint, you can easily see how jealousy could have crept into the situation. It would probably be better to say they were counterparts. Paul was a scholar. His training prepared him for such, and we see it in his speeches and in his prolific writing. Simon Peter, on the other hand, seems to be more a man of action. His limited authorship, although it has flashes of brilliance, is more practical in nature.

One significant test of their relationship had to be when Paul confronted Simon Peter "to his face" about his hypocrisy regarding certain Gentiles (Galatians chapter 2). From every indication, Simon Peter received the rebuke and made the appropriate corrections. Hooray for Paul, for doing the right thing! And hooray for Simon Peter, for responding in the right way!

The ultimate proof of Simon Peter's admiration for Paul comes at the end of his second letter. He commends Paul as "our beloved brother," and for his "wisdom" shown in all his writings. He comments that some of the things Paul says are "hard to understand." (No disagreement there!) And he chastises those who twist Paul's words, as they do "the other scriptures." Interestingly, Simon Peter is thus the first to acknowledge a new era of Scripture writing is occurring at that time. By his kind words for his counterpart Paul, it is pleasant to see Simon Peter's growth as a man of character and humility.

134

I've already mentioned my love for Stanley Shipp, my coworker in the gospel, mentor, and friend. It's incredible, all that I learned from him. But I learned another important thing by working with him, and that is that I couldn't be him. Stanley had incredible charisma. He drew people like a magnet. Fortunately, he was always very mature about this. Thankfully, he chose to be a servant of the Lord and not a cult leader! While I am not devoid of charisma, I began to realize I was given only a fraction of what he had in terms of being a people person. I will admit it took a while to work through my feelings on this. But with the Lord's help, I began to accept Stanley's gifts for what they were, and mine in the same way. At the same time, Stanley respected some things I could do in ministry that he couldn't, and wasn't reluctant to create opportunities or point me in those directions. For example, I often joked that Stanley was "the best sit-on-the-floor Bible teacher" in the world (which in his humility, he dismissed adamantly!). His verse-by-verse studies to young people are legend. Yet, he sometimes felt limited in the introduction phase of teaching a book of the Bible – things about the author, the original recipients, the purpose of the book, etc. So when a new study was starting with some group of young people there in St. Louis, he would ask me to do the introduction. And since he was frequently out of town for speaking appointments, I taught many classes in his absence. Now after his passing, I am so thankful that we, due in large part to his wisdom, struck this balance as coworkers in the gospel. Jealousy didn't hinder our work or spoil our friendship.

Reality check: you won't work long in Christian service, paid or volunteer, until there'll be someone with whom you will be compared, or with whom you will have to share an area of ministry. If so, imitate the attitude of Simon Peter. Also, remember these two related Scriptures: "For where you have envy and selfish ambition, there you will find disorder, and every evil practice" (James 3:16) and "Do nothing from selfishness, or conceit, but in humility count others better than yourselves" (Philippians 2:3).

"With the help of Silas, whom I regard as a faithful brother, I have written to you briefly, encouraging you and testifying that this is the true grace of God. Stand fast in it." (1st Peter 5:12)

d. Be Sure You Remember

The latter part of Simon Peter's life is not recorded in Scripture. Traditions abound about his travels, home base, and death. It has never been historically confirmed, for example, whether or not he actually lived and served as a "bishop"(elder) in Rome. Many believe, based solely upon tradition, he was, at his own request, crucified upside down. This, at least, would have been consistent with the humility he seems to have developed as he matured in Christ. He surely would have felt unworthy to die in the same way as his Lord.

What we do know is 15-20 years after we leave Simon Peter in Acts chapter 15, he wrote two short books. These were preserved, and are now in our New Testament as 1st Peter and 2nd Peter. Even if he wasn't identified as the author, many would quickly figure out it was Simon Peter. You can see him in almost every line! He seems in a hurry, he jumps from subject to subject, but he comes back again and again to a few very basic themes. He can't seem to do enough to honor Jesus Christ. Nor can he be more fervent in his call for steadfastness by those of "like precious faith" (2 Peter 1:1) For one who was "ordinary, uneducated," (Acts 4:13) he shows some rather profound theological insights!

One of the most fascinating aspects of Simon Peter's last book (and therefore his last message to us) is his emphasis on remembering. In 2 Peter 1:12-15 he promises to always remind them of the truths he's been sharing. He states the validity of his doing so while he is still alive. And finally he promises to make every effort to continue to remind us after his departure. Now how could he do that, except through the things he wrote? It's not difficult to see how much Simon Peter wanted his readers to continually read his writings, so as to never forget these vital truths. This principle is true of all Scripture – if we stop reading and listening to the Word of God, we will forget. And if we forget, we'll make ourselves vulnerable to all kinds of spiritual disaster.

I've already discussed the importance of remembering spiritual things that have happened in your life. Let me share one last precious memory of mine.

When I was about ten years old, my Daddy made an unexpected announcement to the family. He said we were going to read from the gospel of John each evening before bedtime. I remember it as if it were yesterday. I remember where we gathered in the living room – my parents were on the couch and my sister and I sat on the floor. And thus we positioned ourselves for twenty-one successive nights. Daddy read; we listened. No commentary, no teaching – just the simple reading of God's Word. We had never done anything like that before. We never did anything like it again. But the impact on me was profound!

The three weeks of bedtime readings stand out in my memory as perhaps the singularly most important memory of my childhood. Sometimes people ask me today why I love to preach and teach so much from the gospel of John. Or they ask me why I think it is so important to read the Bible at home with your family, particularly when children are in the impressionable years.

I don't know what compelled my father to do this. And although I could still ask, I think I won't. Some things are just better left unanswered.

What precious memories do you cherish? Experiences, whether great or small, that somehow dramatically shaped the rest of your spiritual life? You might even consider writing these memories on paper or into a computer file. Don't be reluctant to be detailed, even colorful, as you write your memories. Remember as best you can the names, faces, and sights, smells, and sounds surrounding your memories. As you write, expect to find yourself smiling some and shedding a few tears.

I recently presented some of this material about Simon Peter at a seminar in Prague, the Czech Republic. We know missionaries there, and they were hopeful there would be some interest in the subject matter. But with me as the speaker, it was going to have to be for those who could understand English. There was a nice response, both by local members and a few others, who could, more or less, understand my speech (albeit the Southern variety of American English!). I was particularly struck by the response of one young woman who attended the seminar. She said she had always thought of the Apostle Peter as someone "old and wise," but certainly not the one she'd just been hearing about, especially in those early stories.

Thankfully by the time we come to the end of things revealed about or written by Simon Peter, we do in fact see him as "old and wise." But getting there was quite a journey, wouldn't you say!

And what will you remember about Simon Peter? I hope you will remember some of the stories showing his tendencies, which may have reminded you of yourself, and how these weaknesses were turned into strengths. I hope you'll remember how he wanted those of us who read his writings to continually study the Scriptures.

But hopefully most of all, I hope you'll remember a man who learned, over a lifetime, to love Jesus Christ above all else.

"So I will always remind you of these things, even though you know them and are firmly established in the truth you now have." (2nd Peter 1:12)